The Farmer's Daughters

Recipes from Our Childhood — Worth Remembering and Sharing

Martha

Mary

Flora

1987	1st Printing	5,000
1993	2nd Printing	3,000
2001	3rd Printing	5,000

ISBN 0-96207440-3

Printed in the USA by

WIMMER
The Wimmer Companies
Memphis

1-800-548-2537

INTRODUCTION

The idea for this cookbook originated in December of 1986 when two sisters, Martha Merritt and Mary Mayfield, started trying to think of a way to help the Multiple Sclerosis Society in it's fight against this disease. Their older sister, Flora, had been diagnosed in November of 1985 as having MS. Flora is one of the fortunate ones, seemingly having a mild bout; however, after reading and learning more about MS, they realized that not everyone is so fortunate. The younger sisters had a desire to do something. Serious thoughts were given to the cookbook, and in April of 1987, they told Flora what they had in mind. She loved the idea!

Being Farmer's Daughters, they all had learned to cook at an early age. They were reared on a small farm in the Point DeLuce community, located approximately twelve miles southeast of DeWitt, Arkansas. Since there were no boys in the family, they had each done their share of farm chores---from gathering the eggs, to helping their dad in the rice fields, to helping their mother can and freeze garden vegetables for the winter months.

Even though much thought and work has gone into this cookbook, it was fun, and all are excited about sharing their recipes with others. Hopefully everyone who purchases or receives this book will enjoy using it and also know they are helping in the fight to conquer Multiple Sclerosis.

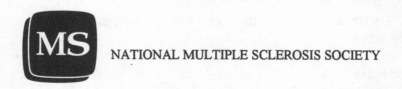 NATIONAL MULTIPLE SCLEROSIS SOCIETY

$1.00 from the sale of this book will be given to the National Multiple Sclerosis Society.

WHAT IS MULTIPLE SCLEROSIS?

Multiple Sclerosis is a chronic, often disabling disease of the central nervous system. Symptoms may be mild such as numbness in the limbs or severe symptoms such as paralysis or loss of vision.

Most people with MS are diagnosed between the ages of 20 and 40 but the unpredictable physical and emotional effects can be lifelong. The progress, severity and specific symptoms of MS in any one person cannot yet be predicted, but advances in research and treatment are giving hope to those affected by the disease.

An estimated 250,000 to 350,000 Americans have multiple sclerosis. The National Multiple Sclerosis Society is dedicated to ending the devastating effects of multiple sclerosis.

We still do not know the cause of or the cure for Multiple Sclerosis. Those questions are the subject of intensive research on a national and an international scale. The National Multiple Sclerosis Society is the only national voluntary health organization in the United States devoted to supporting national and international research on multiple sclerosis. Society members are people with MS, their family members, concerned friends, neighbors and healthcare professionals.

Information, local referrals, publications, and programs are available from the National Multiple Sclerosis Society and its 50-state network of chapters. These chapters offer a variety of services which include education, referral and information, newly diagnosed support, lending library, research, newsletters, self-help groups, peer support, advocacy and more.

For more information or to reach the chapter nearest you, call 1-800-FIGHT-MS (1-800-344-4867) and select Option #1. You can visit the Society's web site at www.nmss.org.

This information furnished by the National Multiple Sclerosis Society, Arkansas Division.

DEDICATION
To The Farmer And His Wife

ACKNOWLEDGMENTS

We wish to express our sincere thanks to persons for the following:

Cover - Original Water Color by Lyda Laneville.

Illustrations - Martha Merritt.

Those special friends for their assistance in many ways, especially on "Cookbook Eve".

Their help and support is greatly appreciated.

TABLE OF CONTENTS

OTHER DESIRABLES

Appetizers

APPETIZERS

ARTICHOKE SPREAD

1 can artichoke hearts, drained
1 cup mayonnaise
3/4 cup parmesan cheese

Chop artichoke hearts and mix with other ingredients.
Place in casserole and bake at 350° until hot and
bubbly. Great served with wheat crackers.

AVOCADO DIP

3 avocados, mashed
1 Tablespoon lemon juice
2 Tablespoons lime juice
1 Tablespoon grated onion
1 teaspoon salt
1/4 teaspoon chili powder
1/2 cup mayonnaise
1 small can chopped ripe olives
1/4 cup bacon bits
dash of hot sauce

Mix avocado with lemon and lime juice thoroughly. Add
remaining ingredients. Keep refrigerated. Serve in
chilled bowl.

BACON WRAPPED WATER CHESTNUTS

2 cans whole water chestnuts
3/4 cup soy sauce
granulated sugar
bacon

Marinate water chestnuts in soy sauce for 5 hours,
turning often. Roll in sugar and wrap in 1/2 strip of
bacon without stretching bacon. Secure with toothpick
and bake at 400° for 20-25 minutes or until bacon
starts getting crisp. Serve hot. (Chicken livers may
be used instead of water chestnuts).

CHEESE DIP

1 pound processed cheese
1 can chili, without beans
1 can tamales, chopped
3 Tablespoons minced onion

Melt cheese in double boiler or microwave. Add other ingredients, stir and heat until very warm.

CHILI CON QUESO

1 4-oz. can whole green chiles
2 tomatoes, peeled and diced
1 teaspoon seasoned salt
1 teaspoon instant minced onion
1/2 pound processed cheese, cubed
1/4 cup milk

Drain, chop, and remove seeds from chiles. In saucepan, cook tomatoes, chiles, onions, and salt for 15 minutes. Add cheese and milk and cook slowly until melted. Be sure heat is low, mixture will scorch easily.

CHIPPED BEEF DIP

2 8-oz. packages cream cheese
1 8-oz. carton sour cream
1 teaspoon milk
1 banana pepper or 1 bell pepper, minced
1/2 cup onion, finely chopped
2 packages (2½-oz.) smoked beef
1/2 jalapeno pepper, finely chopped

Cut beef in fine strips, then chop. Mix all ingredients together and pour in large pie plate. Bake at 350° for 45 minutes. Chopped nuts can be sprinkled on top. Serve hot. Best when served with nacho cheese tortilla chips.

11

CHOCOLATE FONDUE

1 package milk chocolate candy kisses
1/2 cup light corn syrup
1/4 cup butter
1 teaspoon vanilla
3 Tablespoons milk

Melt chocolate in fondue pot, add other ingredients
and mix well. Great dipped with fruit--especially
bananas, apples, and strawberries.

CRAB BALLS

1 Tablespoon butter
1 Tablespoon flour
1/2 cup milk
1 cup crab meat
1/2 teaspoon salt
1/2 cup cornstarch

Melt butter over medium heat then add flour stirring
constantly. Add milk slowly, and cook until
thickened. Bring to a boil and add meat and salt.
Chill. Make small balls. Roll in cornstarch and deep
fry. Good served with oriental sauces.

CREAM CHEESE MOLD

1 envelope unflavored gelatin
1/3 cup cold water
6 small packages cream cheese
1 Tablespoon milk
1 pint whipping cream, whipped
2 Tablespoons celery hearts, finely chopped
2 Tablespoons green pepper, finely chopped
2 teaspoons onion, finely chopped
2 Tablespoons catsup
Dash of hot sauce

Soak gelatin in water and dissolve in double boiler.
Cream together milk and cheese, and mix with gelatin.
Add other ingredients in order given and pour in oiled
mold and refrigerate.

DRUNK WIENERS

2 pounds wieners, cut in fourths
1/2 cup brown sugar
3/4 cup whiskey
1½ cups catsup
1/2 cup water
2 Tablespoons minced onion

Combine all ingredients in saucepan and bring to a boil. Lower heat and simmer covered for 1 hour. These should be kept hot during serving. Crock pot or chafing dish works well for this.

HOT LINKS

4 pounds all beef hotdogs
2 teaspoons salt
1½ cups sugar
1 teaspoon pepper
1/4 cup cumin or 1 teaspoon cumin powder
1 jar hot peppers
2 cups chopped onion
1 quart red wine vinegar

Cut hotdogs in half. Bring remaining ingredients to a boil and add hotdogs. Turn heat down and simmer for about 30 minutes.

LAYERED MEXICAN DIP

2 ripe avocados
1/2 cup onion, finely chopped
1 16-oz. carton sour cream
1 small jar picanti sauce
1 8-oz. package mozzarella cheese, grated
1 Tablespoon lemon juice

Mash avocados, add onions, and mix with lemon juice to keep from turning dark. Layer 1/2 avocados, 1/2 sour cream, 1/2 picanti sauce, and 1/2 cheese; repeat. Best if this sets at least 4 hours before serving.

MARY'S CHEESEBALL

1 8-oz. package cream cheese
1 tube garlic cheese
1 teaspoon salt
1 teaspoon Worcestershire sauce
1/2 cup parmesan cheese
1 teaspoon chili powder
chopped nuts

All ingredients should be room temperature. Mix together in order, blending with each ingredient. Form into ball and roll in chopped nuts.

MEX SPREAD

1 large can bean dip
Blend together: 2 Tablespoons lemon juice
                3 ripe avocados
                1/2 teaspoon salt
                1/4 teaspoon pepper
Blend together: 1 8-oz. carton sour cream
                1/2 cup mayonnaise
                1/2 package taco seasoning
Mix together: 1 bunch green onions, chopped
                3 tomatoes, peeled and chopped
                1 small can chopped black olives
                1 8oz. package cheddar cheese, grated

Layer: Bean dip on bottom. Avocado mix second. Sour cream mix third. Cheese and onion mix last. Make this in a large round tray with shallow sides.

14

MEXICAN DIP

1 small can chopped ripe olives
2 large tomatoes, peeled and chopped
5 green onions, chopped
1 small can green chiles, chopped
3 Tablespoons oil
2 Tablespoons vinegar
1 teaspoon garlic salt

Combine all ingredients in a bowl and let set in refrigerator overnight. Drain well and serve with tortilla chips.

PARTY PIZZAS

1 pound sausage
1 pound ground chuck
1 pound processed cheese
1 teaspoon oregano
1 teaspoon garlic salt
1 teaspoon Worcestershire sauce
2 loaves party rye bread

Brown meats together. Drain well. Add remaining ingredients and cook until cheese melts. Remove from stove and spread on party rye. Place on cookie sheet and cook at 400° in oven for 10 minutes. These may be frozen individually then placed in plastic bags.

PIZZA APPETIZERS

1 pound ground beef
1 pound mild sausage
1 pound processed cheese
1 teaspoon basil
1/4 teaspoon garlic powder
1 teaspoon oregano
1 Tablespoon dried parsley

Brown meats separately and drain. Combine all ingredients with meat and put on party rye. Top with parmesan cheese. Bake for 15 minutes at 325°.

SAUSAGE BALLS

1 pound sausage
1 pound cheddar cheese, grated
3 cups biscuit mix

Start with ingredients at room temperature. Mix all together thoroughly with hands then roll in 3/4-inch balls and place on cookie sheet. Bake at 350° until light brown. These may be frozen, stored in bags, and cooked as needed. Serve hot.

SHRIMP DIP

1/2 pound mild cheddar cheese
1 can shrimp
1/4 cup onion
1 cup mayonnaise
1 teaspoon Worcestershire sauce

Grate cheese, shrimp, and onion (or put in food processor). Add mayonnaise and Worcestershire sauce. Mix well and refrigerate until ready to serve.

SPINACH DIP

2 packages frozen chopped spinach
1 bunch green onions, finely chopped
1/3 cup mayonnaise
2 Tablespoons lemon juice
1/4 teaspoon salt
2 hard-boiled eggs, chopped
1½ cups sour cream
1 Tablespoon prepared mustard
Dash each: hot sauce and garlic powder

Cook spinach according to package directions. Squeeze out all water. Add onions and eggs and mix with other ingredients. Cover and refrigerate overnight.

TAMALE DIP

1 Tablespoon grated onion
1 can chili (no beans)
1 can tamales (mashed)
1/2 pound grated American cheese

Mix together, put in casserole dish and bake at 350°
until thoroughly heated.

TURKEY PATE

left over turkey, deboned
mayonnaise
salt and pepper

Put through food processor until finely ground. Salt
and pepper to taste. Add enough mayonnaise to mix
thoroughly and for desired consistency. This is so
good and so simple.

VEGETABLE DIP

1 cup mayonnaise
1 cup sour cream
2 Tablespoons dill weed or
1 Tablespoon dill seed
2 Tablespoons minced onion
2 Tablespoons parsley
2 Tablespoons seasoned salt

Mix 12 hours in advance of serving. Refrigerate.
Serve with fresh vegetables.

OTHER DESIRABLES

Soups

BEEF STEW

2 pounds stew meat
2 Tablespoons oil
3 cups tomatoes
1 bay leaf
6 potatoes
4 carrots
6 medium onions

Cut meat into 1 inch cubes, flour and brown. Add tomatoes, bay leaf, salt and pepper and simmer for 45 minutes. Cut vegetables in large pieces and add to meat mixture. Cover and simmer till vegetables are tender. Can be thickened with water and cornstarch if desired.

CAL'S CHEESE SOUP

2 carrots, finely chopped
2 stalks celery, finely chopped
1 onion, finely chopped
2½ pounds processed cheese, chunked
2 quarts water
6 chicken bouillon cubes
1 cup softened butter

Dissolve bouillon cubes in 2 quarts hot water. Add butter, then other ingredients and cook slowly for 45 minutes. If too thick, add one cup water.

CHEESY BROCCOLI SOUP

1/3 cup onions
1 Tablespoon butter
2¼ cups milk
1 8-oz. package cream cheese
3/4 pound processed cheese spread
1 10-oz. package frozen chopped broccoli
1/8 teaspoon ground nutmeg

Cook broccoli by package directions and drain. Cook onions in butter until tender. Add milk and cream cheese. Stir over medium heat until cheese melts. Add other ingredients and heat thoroughly. Stir occasionally but watch closely.

CHILI

2 pounds ground chuck
3 medium onions, chopped
1 large can kidney beans
1 large can tomatoes
1 Tablespoon chili powder
2 cups water

Brown ground chuck with onions. Put in sauce pan with other ingredients, cover and simmer for 45 minutes.

CLAM CHOWDER

4 medium potatoes
1 large onion
4 tomatoes
1 carrot
25 clams
4 Tablespoons butter
salt and pepper

Finely chop all vegetables and clams. Cook vegetables in 2 quarts water until done. Add clams, butter and season to taste.

CREAM OF CELERY SOUP

4 cups finely cut celery
2 cups chicken broth
2 cups boiling water
1/2 cup minced onion
2 Tablespoons butter
3 Tablespoons flour
2½ cups milk
1 8-oz. carton whipping cream
1 teaspoon seasoned salt

Cook celery in broth and water until tender. Put through a blender. Saute onions in butter until clear, add flour and milk. Cook, stirring constantly until thickened. Add celery mixture, cream and salt. Simmer until hot.

21

CREAMY TOMATO SOUP

1 16-oz. can tomatoes
1 onion, chopped
1 cup water
1/4 teaspoon soda
3 cups milk
2 Tablespoons butter
1 teaspoon salt
1/4 teaspoon pepper

Cook tomatoes and onions in water till thick. Cool slightly and put through a blender. Add soda. Heat milk until very hot then remove from heat. When milk and tomatoes are the same temperature, add tomatoes to milk gradually, beating constantly. Add butter, salt and pepper. This is very good but must be carefully made to keep mixture from curdling.

EASIEST EVER VEGETABLE SOUP

3 medium potatoes, cubed
2 medium cans mixed vegetables
1 small onion, chopped
1 pound ground chuck
1 large can tomato juice

Brown meat and onion together. Drain. Put meat, onion, tomato juice and mixed vegetables (not drained) in large stew pot. Let simmer while cooking potatoes in just enough water to keep them from sticking. When potatoes are tender, mash three or four times and add to soup. Let simmer for 30 minutes. The potatoes will thicken the soup slightly. Serve over hot cornbread.

MINESTRONE

1 cup dried navy beans
8 cups water
1 Tablespoon salt
1/4 teaspoon pepper
3/4 cup celery, diced
1/8 teaspoon minced garlic
1/2 cup olive oil
2 cans tomatoes
1/4 cup parsley, chopped
2½ cups cabbage, shredded
1 small zucchini, chopped
1 cup small shell macaroni
1/4 cup parmesan cheese

Cook beans until done after soaking overnight in the 8 cups of water. Saute onion and celery in olive oil and add to beans along with tomatoes and parsley. Simmer for 40 minutes. Add cabbage, squash, macaroni, and parmesan cheese. Simmer another 30 minutes.

NAVY BEAN SOUP

1 cup diced ham
2 cups dried navy beans
1 cup onion, chopped
1/2 cup celery, chopped
2 cups tomatoes, chopped
4 slices bacon, cooked and crumbled

Soak beans overnight in water. Cook beans, ham, onion, celery, and tomatoes until beans start to get tender. Add bacon and simmer for 1½ hours. Cover for 45 minutes then uncover and cook the last 45 minutes. Salt and pepper to taste.

ONION SOUP

5 large yellow onions, thinly sliced
1/3 cup butter
4 cups beef bouillon
2 teaspoons salt
1 teaspoon pepper
1 teaspoon Worcestershire sauce

Saute onions in butter slowly for 30 to 40 minutes stirring occasionally. Add bouillon, salt, pepper and worchestershire sauce. Simmer for 1½ hours.

POTATO SOUP

6 medium potatoes
1 carrot, very finely chopped
1 stalk celery, very finely chopped
1 beef bouillon cube dissolved in 1/2 cup hot water
1/4 cup baked ham, finely chopped

Cook above ingredients together in enough water to cover. Bring to a boil, lower heat and simmer until potatoes start to thicken. Mash once or twice with potato masher to help thicken.

POTATO AND CORNED BEEF SOUP

6 medium potatoes
1 large onion, chopped
1 small can corned beef

Dice potatoes and cook with onions in water until potatoes are tender and they start to thicken themselves. Add corned beef and simmer for 15 to 20 minutes. Salt and pepper to taste.

SPLIT PEA SOUP

1 pound split peas
2½ quarts hot water
1 cup ham pieces
1/8 teaspoon minced garlic
1/2 cup onion, chopped
1/4 cup celery, chopped
salt and pepper

Mix all ingredients. Bring to a boil, reduce heat and simmer for 1½ hours.

VEGETABLE SOUP

6 to 8 cups water
1 onion, chopped
1 cup chopped carrots
1 cup green beans
1 cup corn
1 cup potatoes
2 cups tomato juice
Salt and pepper to taste

Mix all ingredients except corn. Cook until tender and add corn. Simmer for 45 minutes. Meat can be added if desired.

GREAT NORTHERN BEAN CHILI

1 pound ground beef
1 onion, chopped
2 16-oz. cans great northern beans
2 cans tomatoes
1 teaspoon oregano
chili powder to taste
1 teaspoon brown sugar
2 Tablespoons catsup

Brown ground beef and onion together in skillet. Drain and add beans, tomatoes, oregano, catsup and chili powder. Mix well. Simmer 15 to 20 minutes. Add brown sugar. Salt and pepper to taste.

OTHER DESIRABLES

Sauces and Gravies

GRANDMA LUCY'S CHOCOLATE GRAVY

1/4 cup cocoa
3/4 cup sugar
1 Tablespoon flour
3 Tablespoons light corn syrup
3 Tablespoons water
1/2 cup evaporated milk

Mix everything except milk in saucepan and cook over medium heat, stirring constantly, until a boil is reached. Boil and stir 1 minute. Remove from heat and stir in milk. Beat for a minute. Pour over hot biscuits and top with a pat of butter.

GIBLET GRAVY

1 quart broth, chicken, turkey or duck
2 hard-boiled eggs, sliced
1 each: liver, gizzard, heart, cooked and chopped
1 teaspoon salt
1/4 teaspoon pepper
1/4 cup onion, finely chopped
1/4 cup celery, finely chopped
1/4 cup butter
3 Tablespoons cornstarch
1/2 cup water

Saute onion and celery in butter. Bring broth to a boil, add eggs, meats, salt, pepper, and onion and celery mixture. Mix cornstarch in 1/2 cup water. Pour in half of cornstarch mixture and stir. Pour other half in slowly, stopping when you have desired thickness.

MILK GRAVY

6 Tablespoons meat drippings
4 Tablespoons flour
1 teaspoon salt
1/4 teaspoon pepper
1½ cups milk
1/2 cup water

Stir flour into heated drippings. Let brown and add milk and water while stirring over high heat. More milk may be needed to achieve desired consistency. Salt and pepper, turn heat to low and cook for 3-5 minutes.

BARBEQUE SAUCE

1 cup vinegar
1 cup catsup
2 cups water
1 teaspoon prepared mustard
2 Tablespoons chili powder
1/2 teaspoon red pepper
1/2 cup molasses

Mix together and refrigerate. This is better if it sets for several days.

BEARNAISE SAUCE

3 egg yolks
1½ Tablespoons tarragon vinegar
3 Tablespoons cream
dash of salt
dash cayenne pepper
5 Tablespoons oil
2½ Tablespoons chopped fresh herbs
dash garlic powder

Combine egg yolks, vinegar, cream, salt and cayenne pepper. Cook in double boiler until thickened, beating constantly. Add oil, herbs and garlic. Mix well.

SAUCES AND GRAVIES

CHEESE SAUCE

1 Tablespoon butter
1 Tablespoon flour
1/2 teaspoon dry mustard
1/4 teaspoon salt
1 cup evaporated milk
1 cup processed cheese, grated
dash pepper

Melt butter and add flour, dry mustard, salt, and pepper. Stir in milk and cook over medium heat, stirring constantly until mixture thickens. Add cheese and stir until melted.

CHILI SAUCE

1 gallon tomatoes, peeled
1 dozen medium onions
6 green peppers
3 Tablespoons salt
2 teaspoons black pepper
2 teaspoons red pepper
1/2 teaspoon cloves
1/2 teaspoon allspice
1/2 teaspoon cinnamon
2 cups sugar
3/4 cup vinegar

Chop vegetables and add remaining ingredients. Cook slowly for 3 to 4 hours or until thick. Pour in sterile jars and seal. This is very hot! For milder sauce use one teaspoon each of black and red pepper.

CRANBERRY SAUCE

1 quart cranberries
1 pint water
1 pint sugar

Boil sugar and water for five minutes. Add cranberries and boil for 15 minutes. Take off burner and let set for 1 hour.

CHOCOLATE SAUCE

1 cup cocoa
1½ cups sugar
1 cup hot water
2 teaspoons vanilla
dash of salt

Mix sugar, salt, and cocoa dry. Add sufficient water to make a paste, then add remainder of water. Bring to a boil, stirring constantly. Boil 3 minutes and add vanilla. Pour at once into jar. When cold, place in refrigerator. Makes two cups sauce.

HOLLANDAISE SAUCE

1/2 cup butter
3 egg yolks
2 Tablespoons lemon juice
3 drops hot sauce
1/4 teaspoon salt

Heat butter in saucepan to bubbling; do not scorch. Put all other ingredients in blender and blend at low speed. Take off cover and pour in hot butter slowly while blender is on low speed. Blend only until all butter has been poured into blender.

MUSTARD SAUCE

1 Tablespoon prepared mustard
1 Tablespoon cider vinegar
1/8 teaspoon salt
dash pepper
2 drops hot sauce
1 cup mayonnaise

Mix together in order given. More hot sauce may be used if you like extremely hot mustard sauce.

31

SEAFOOD SAUCE

1 can tomato sauce
1/2 cup chili sauce
1/4 teaspoon garlic powder
1/4 teaspoon oregano
1/4 teaspoon hot pepper sauce
1/4 teaspoon sugar

Combine all ingredients and simmer for 15 minutes, stirring 3 or 4 times.

SHRIMP COCKTAIL SAUCE

1 cup catsup
1 cup chili sauce
1 Tablespoon vinegar
3 Tablespoons lemon juice
3 Tablespoons Worcestershire sauce
1 teaspoon salt
2 teaspoons horseradish

Put all in quart jar and shake until thoroughly mixed.

SHRIMP SAUCE

1 cup ketchup
1½ teaspoons Worcestershire sauce
1/2 teaspoon hot sauce
1/2 teaspoon horseradish
1 Tablespoon lemon juice
garlic powder to taste

Combine all ingredients together and chill.

SWEET AND SOUR PLUM SAUCE

1 Tablespoon prepared mustard
4 Tablespoons plum jelly

Mix together thoroughly. Other jellies may be used for different flavor. This is good for chicken nuggets.

TARTER SAUCE

1/2 cup mayonnaise
1½ Tablespoons sweet relish
1 Tablespoon lemon juice
1/4 teaspoon Worcestershire sauce
1/4 teaspoon finely chopped parsley
1 teaspoon grated onion

Mix all together and chill till ready to serve.

TARTER SAUCE

1/2 cup mayonnaise
1 Tablespoon pickle relish
1 Tablespoon lemon juice
3 Tablespoons ketchup
2 teaspoons finely chopped onion

Mix all together. More ketchup can be added if desired. Keep refrigerated until ready to serve.

WHITE SAUCE

2 Tablespoons butter
2 Tablespoons flour
1/2 teaspoon salt
1/8 teaspoon pepper
1 cup milk

Melt butter; Stir in flour and cook until bubbling. Slowly add milk, stirring constantly until boils. Add seasonings.

33

OTHER DESIRABLES

Salads
and
Salad Dressings

BLACKBERRY SALAD

1 package grape gelatin
2 cups hot water
2 cups frozen whipped topping
3 cups fresh blackberries
1/2 cup chopped pecans

Dissolve gelatin in hot water. Chill until almost set then beat until light and foamy. Fold in whipped topping, nuts and blackberries. Refrigerate until set.

BLUEBERRY SALAD

2 small packages black cherry gelatin
2 cups hot water
1 can crushed pineapple, drained
1 can blueberries, drain 1/2 juice
1 8-oz. package cream cheese
1/2 cup sour cream
1/4 cup sugar
1 cup chopped nuts

Dissolve gelatin in hot water, add pineapple and blueberries. Pour in 2 quart casserole and chill to set. Combine remaining ingredients and spread over gelatin. Sprinkle a few crushed nuts over top.

CURRIED FRUIT

1 can peach halves
1 can pineapple chunks
1 can pear halves
1 jar cherries
1/2 cup butter
3/4 cup light brown sugar
4 teaspoons curry powder

Drain fruit and soak on paper towels to remove all moisture. Put in casserole dish. Melt butter and mix together with brown sugar and curry powder. Pour over fruit and stir lightly. Bake 1 hour at 325°. Serve warm. This may be reheated.

CRANBERRY SALAD

3 cups cranberries, crushed
1-3/4 cups sugar
1 package raspberry gelatin
1 package strawberry gelatin
1½ cups nuts, chopped

Mix cranberries and sugar and let set overnight.
Dissolve gelatin by package directions and add other
ingredients. Refrigerate until ready to serve.

MOM'S CRANBERRY SALAD

1 can jellied cranberry sauce, cubed
3 bananas, cubed
1 15-oz. can crushed pineapple, drained
1 9-oz. carton frozen whipped topping
1/2 cup sugar
1 cup nuts, chopped
2 Tablespoons lemon juice
2 drops red food coloring (optional)

Stir cubed bananas in lemon juice to keep from turning
dark.   Fold all ingredients together gently.   Freeze
in 9X13 pan.

FAVORITE FRUIT SALAD

1 can fruit cocktail
1 can chunk pineapple
1 can mandarin oranges
1 jar cherries
1 cup small marshmallows
1 cup chopped pecans
1 8-oz. carton sour cream

Drain all fruit and mix together with other
ingredients. Refrigerate overnight before serving.

CHERRY 'N COLA SALAD

1 package cherry gelatin
1 package strawberry gelatin
1 cup chopped nuts
1 8-oz. package cream cheese
1 can crushed pineapple
1 cup boiling water
1 cup cola
1/2 cup sour cream
1 can dark sweet cherries

Blend cream cheese and sour cream. Dissolve gelatin in water and add cheese mixture. Blend well. Drain fruit juices together and save 1½ cups juice. Add juice and cola to gelatin mixture and chill until almost set. Fold in nuts and fruits. Chill until firm. Makes attractive gelatin mold.

FROZEN SALAD

1 can sweetened condensed milk
1 carton frozen whipped topping
1 small can crushed pineapple
1 cup chopped nuts
1 package frozen strawberries or cherries

Mix together and freeze.

COTTAGE CHEESE SALAD

1 9-oz. carton frozen whipped topping
1 box strawberry gelatin, dry
1 8-oz. carton cottage cheese
1 can crushed pineapple
1 jar cherries, cut in half
1 cup nuts

Mix topping, gelatin and cottage cheese. Let set five minutes, stirring occasionally. Add fruit and nuts and refrigerate.

FRUIT SALAD

1 can peach pie filling
1 can pineapple chunks, drained
  or one can mandarin oranges
2 or 3 sliced bananas
1 small box frozen strawberries

Mix well and refrigerate until ready to serve.

ORANGE SALAD

2 cups water
1 small can frozen orange juice
1 small package lemon gelatin
1 small package orange gelatin
1 large can crushed pineapple, drained
1 can mandarin oranges, drained

Boil water and orange juice. Pour over gelatin. Add pineapple and oranges. Refrigerate until solid.

ORANGE PINEAPPLE SALAD

1 9-oz. carton frozen whipped topping
1 8-oz. carton cottage cheese
1 medium can crushed pineapple, drained
1 can mandarin oranges, drained and cut in half
1 box orange gelatin, dry

Mix together and chill. Better if chilled overnight.

PEACH WHIP

2 small packages peach gelatin
2 cups boiling water
1 small can peaches, drained and diced
2 cups ice cubes
1 cup frozen whipped topping

Pour boiling water over gelatin and dissolve. Stir in ice cubes and refrigerate until almost set. Remove and stir in whipped topping, blending well. Add peaches and mix well. Transfer to serving dish and garnish with whipped topping, peaches, nuts, etc. Keep refrigerated.

PEAR SALAD

1 large can pear halves
1 package cherry gelatin, or
1 package lime gelatin
water

Lay pear halves flat side down in glass casserole dish. Dissolve gelatin as per directions on package and pour over pears; refrigerate until set. Take pear juice adding enough water to make 1½ cups liquid and bring to a rolling boil. Pour over gelatin and pears. When ready to serve, cut in squares around pears and place on salad plate flat side of pear up. Fill pear centers with any chopped fruit, cottage cheese, chicken salad, sherbet, or anything you desire.

STRAWBERRY-CREAM SQUARES

2 3-oz. packages strawberry gelatin
2 cups boiling water
2 10-oz. packages frozen strawberries
1 13½-oz. can crushed pineapple, drained
2 large ripe bananas, finely diced
1 8-oz. carton sour cream

Dissolve gelatin in boiling water. Mix in other ingredients except sour cream. Pour 1/2 mixture into an 8X8 pan. Chill until firm. Spread sour cream evenly and pour remaining gelatin mixture on top. Chill until firm. Top with sour cream.

STRAWBERRY SALAD

2 packages strawberry gelatin
1 cup boiling water
1 can crushed pineapple, drained
1 8-oz. carton sour cream
2 mashed bananas
2 10-oz. packages frozen strawberries
1 cup chopped nuts

Dissolve gelatin in water. Add other ingredients except sour cream. Divide into two bowls and chill until partially set. Spread sour cream over one half and top with other half of gelatin mixture.

STRAWBERRY COTTAGE CHEESE SALAD

1 package strawberry gelatin
1 cup boiling water
1/2 cup cottage cheese
1 small jar cherries, drained
1 can crushed pineapple, drained
1/2 cup chopped nuts
1/2 pint whipping cream

Mix gelatin and water, refrigerate until mixture starts to thicken. Mix ingredients in order given folding in whipped cream. Refrigerate.

41

WHIPPED CHERRY CREAM

1 large can cherry pie filling
1 can crushed pineapple, drained
1 can sweetened condensed milk
1 small container frozen whipped topping
1 cup small marshmallows
1/2 cup chopped pecans

Mix all together in large bowl. Chill in shallow dish
for at least 2 hours.

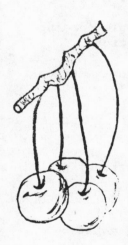

CHICKEN SALAD

2 cups chopped boiled chicken
1/4 cup chopped onion
1/4 cup chopped celery
3 hard-boiled eggs
3/4 cup mayonnaise

Mix ingredients in order and spread on bread. Apples,
white seedless grapes, raisins, celery, or pecans can
be added if desired.

EASIEST EVER HAM SALAD

1 can deviled ham
1 Tablespoon sweet relish
1 Tablespoon minced onion
2 hard-boiled eggs, mashed
1/2 cup mayonnaise

Mix all ingredients and spread on white or wheat
bread. Especially good to cut crust off and cut
in triangles.

TUNA SALAD

1 can tuna
2 hard-boiled eggs, chopped
1/3 cup onions, chopped
1/4 cup dill pickles, chopped
1/4 cup sweet pickles, chopped
1/4 cup celery, chopped
3/4 cup mayonnaise
salt and pepper

Mix together and make sandwiches.

43

DEBBIE'S BEAN SALAD

1 17-oz. can English peas
1 17-oz. can French cut green beans
1 medium onion, chopped
1/2 cup celery, chopped
1 small jar pimentos, chopped

Marinate over night in:

1 cup vinegar
1 cup sugar
1/2 cup oil
2 teaspoons salt

Refrigerate. Drain 1 1/2 hours before serving.

FOUR BEAN SALAD

1 can green beans
1 can wax beans
1 can lima beans
1 can kidney beans

Drain all of the above and combine. Add:

1/3 cup sugar
1 Tablespoon oil
1 onion, diced
1 Tablespoon lemon juice

Mix together well, and refrigerate before serving.

PINTO BEAN SALAD

2 17-oz. cans pinto beans, drained
1/4 cup grated onion
1 teaspoon prepared mustard
1/2 cup mayonnaise
3 hard boiled eggs, chopped
1/4 Tablespoon pickle relish
salt and pepper

Mix together and chill before serving.

EASIEST EVER COLE SLAW

1 head cabbage, finely chopped
1 teaspoon salt
1/4 teaspoon pepper
1 teaspoon sugar
1 cup salad dressing

Mix together and let set one hour before serving.

FROZEN SLAW

Chop or grate one head of cabbage, one bell pepper, one purple onion and two carrots. Add dressing:

DRESSING

1 cup vinegar
1/4 cup water
1 teaspoon each: celery seed and salt
2 cups sugar

Boil the dressing mixture one minute and cool. Pour over vegetables and mix well. Place in freezer containers and freeze. Thaw before serving.

WILTED LETTUCE

6 small bunches bibb lettuce
4 slices bacon
5 medium radishes, sliced
1 bunch green onions, chopped
3/4 cup vinegar
1/2 cup sugar
1/4 cup bacon fat

Fry bacon until crisp. Cut lettuce and mix with onions, radishes, and crumbled bacon. Combine vinegar, sugar, and fat; heat to boiling. Pour liquid over lettuce and toss. Serve immediately.

M.J.'S CABBAGE SLAW

1 head cabbage, coarsely chopped
1 large purple onion in rings
1 large bell pepper in rings
1 cup sugar

Layer above vegetables in oblong glass dish. Pour sugar evenly over them. Mix the following ingredients together and bring to a boil:

1 Tablespoon salt
1 teaspoon celery seed
1 cup vinegar
1 teaspoon dry mustard
3/4 cup salad oil

Pour hot liquid over vegetable mixture and refrigerate 4 hours before serving. Keeps well in refrigerator for up to a week.

MARINATED CABBAGE SLAW

1 head cabbage, shredded
3/4 cup sugar
1 teaspoon dry mustard
1/4 teaspoon pepper
1 cup oil
1 large onion, thinly sliced
1 teaspoon salt
1 teaspoon celery seed
1 cup vinegar

Put cabbage in large mixing bowl, layer onions on top and sprinkle sugar evenly over all. Do not stir. Mix vinegar, oil, & spices in saucepan and heat to a boil. Take off stove and pour over cabbage, cover and let set overnight in refrigerator. Drain before serving.

SPINACH SALAD

Cook 1/2 pound bacon until crisp. Crumble and set aside.

> Combine: 1 cup salad oil
> 1/2 cup dark vinegar
> 3/4 cup sugar
> 2 teaspoons salt
> 1/3 cup catsup

Shake above ingredients in bottle until well mixed.

Mix 2 bunches torn spinach, 2 cups sliced water chestnuts, 1 cup bean sprouts, 1 bunch green onions, and 4 chopped hard-boiled eggs; add bacon bits, pour dressing over and toss.

TUNA STUFFED TOMATO

1 6 1/2-oz. can tuna
2 hard cooked eggs, chopped
1/2 cup sweet pickles, chopped
1/4 cup celery, chopped
1/2 cup onion, chopped
3/4 cup mayonnaise
2 large tomatoes

Mix all ingredients together except tomatoes. Salt and pepper to taste. Peel tomatoes, put in center of plate and cut in eighths being careful not to cut through bottom of tomato. Spoon tuna salad into center of tomato wedges arranging wedges evenly. Lay chopped lettuce around tomato and serve with your favorite salad dressing. Our favorite is Thousand Island or Buttermilk.

MARINATED VEGETABLE SALAD

1 bunch broccoli
1 head cauliflower
2 cans artichoke hearts, quartered
1 can pitted black olives
1 basket cherry tomatoes
1 large bottle Italian dressing
1 cup parmesan cheese

Wash vegetables & break into bite-size pieces; drain well. Mix all ingredients together except parmesan cheese and marinate overnight in refrigerator. Drain, add parmesan cheese, and serve.

ENGLISH PEA SALAD

2 hard-boiled eggs, chopped
1 onion, chopped
1 small jar pimentos, chopped
2 dill pickles, chopped
1 Tablespoon parsley flakes
1 10-oz. can English peas
mayonnaise
paprika to garnish

Add all ingredients together and stir carefully. Use enough mayonnaise and pickle juice to mix well. Salt and pepper to taste. Garnish with paprika and boiled egg slices.

ENGLISH PEA SALAD

1 17-oz. can English peas
2 hard boiled eggs, chopped
1/4 cup diced onion
1/4 cup diced celery
1/4 cup chopped sweet pickles
1/2 cup American cheese, cubed
1/2 cup salad dressing
2 teaspoons each: prepared mustard, vinegar, and sugar.

Mix together; Salt and pepper to taste. Refrigerate.

QUICK CAESAR SALAD

1 head lettuce, broken into bite-size pieces
1/4 cup bacon bits
1 cup seasoned croutons
1/2 cup parmesan cheese

Do not mix salad until ready to serve. Use Caesar Salad dressing on page 53.

CUBED CUKES

3 cucumbers
2 or 3 Tablespoons sugar
Salad dressing

Peel cucumbers and cut in long slices. Remove seeds and dice. Sprinkle sugar on top of cukes and let stand overnight covered in refrigerator. Stir once or twice. Drain off sugar water, add salad dressing (not mayonnaise) and mix. Ready to serve. (Chopped onion may be added.)

TACO SALAD

1 pound ground beef, browned and drained
1 head lettuce, broken into bite-size pieces
2 medium to large tomatoes, peeled and chopped
1/2 cup grated cheddar cheese
1 9-oz. package crushed tortilla chips
1 can red kidney beans, drained
1 8-oz. bottle Thousand Island dressing
hot sauce to taste

Mix all together well. Serve immediately.

TACO SALAD

1 head lettuce
1 bunch green onions
1 pound cheddar cheese, grated
1 pound ground beef
1 6-oz. package tortilla chips
1 can stewed tomatoes
1 package taco sauce
1 can kidney beans

Put first three ingredients in large salad bowl. Brown ground beef, pour off fat and add tomatoes and taco sauce. Simmer 10 minutes. Add meat mixture and crushed chips to salad. Pour Thousand Island or Catalina dressing over all and mix well. Serve immediately.

TOMATO SALAD

6 medium to large tomatoes
2 large bell peppers
1 large onion
2 Tablespoons sugar
2 Tablespoons vinegar
salt and pepper

Dice vegetables. Mix together and sprinkle with sugar, salt and pepper. Add vinegar and stir. This will make it's own juice from the vinegar. Let set several hours and stir at intervals before serving.

LAYERED SALAD

1 head lettuce, broken in bite-size pieces
1 cup chopped celery
1 cup chopped bell pepper
3/4 cup chopped green onions
1 can English peas, drained
3/4 cup boiled egg, chopped
1 pint mayonnaise
2 Tablespoons sugar
3/4 cup parmesan cheese
3/4 cup bacon bits

Layer in large salad bowl in order.   Cover and refrigerate 6 hours before serving.

JENNY'S LAYERED SALAD

1 large head of lettuce
1/2 cup each: onion, bell pepper, & celery
1 can English peas, drained
1 pint mayonnaise, whipped with 2 Tablespoons sugar
3 oz. parmesan cheese
bacon bits

Break lettuce into bite-size pieces and layer in bottom of salad bowl.   Layer finely chopped onion, pepper, celery, and peas. Cover with mayonnaise and sugar.   Sprinkle with cheese.   Cover with bacon bits. Refrigerate for 2 to 4 hours before serving.

MACARONI SALAD

1 cup raw macaroni, cooked and drained
1/2 cup sweet pickles, chopped
3 hard boiled eggs, chopped
3/4 cup celery, chopped
1 medium onion, chopped
1 Tablespoon prepared mustard
3/4 cup mayonnaise
2 Tablespoons vinegar

Rinse macaroni well under cold water, add remaining ingredients.   Refrigerate until ready to serve.

51

FRENCH (SUGAR) DRESSING

1/4 cup sugar
1/3 cup oil
1/3 cup red wine vinegar
1 teaspoon prepared mustard
1 teaspoon salt
dash garlic salt
dash paprika

Pour all ingredients in a pint jar and shake until
well mixed.   This will separate so you will have to
shake before pouring.

GREEN GODDESS DRESSING

1 cup mayonnaise
1/8 teaspoon minced garlic
1/8 cup chives, minced
1/8 cup green onions
1/4 cup parsley, minced
1 Tablespoon lemon juice
1 Tablespoon tarragon vinegar
1/2 teaspoon salt
1/2 teaspoon pepper
1/2 cup sour cream

Combine ingredients in order and mix thoroughly. Keep
refrigerated.

GUACAMOLE DRESSING

1 egg, beaten
1/2 cup olive oil
1 teaspoon dry mustard
1/4 teaspoon hot sauce
1/3 cup lemon juice
1 Tablespoon Worcestershire sauce
1/2 teaspoon salt
3 ripe avocados, diced
1 bunch green onions, chopped
1/8 teaspoon minced garlic
3/4 cup mayonnaise

Blend in food processor or blender until smooth.
Chill before serving over salad.

BUTTERMILK DRESSING MIX

2 teaspoons salt
2 teaspoons garlic powder
3 Tablespoons minced instant onion
1½ teaspoons black pepper
2 teaspoons sugar
1½ teaspoons paprika
1 Tablespoon red pepper flakes

Combine all ingredients together and store in tightly
covered container.

BUTTERMILK DRESSING

1 Tablespoon buttermilk dressing mix
1 cup mayonnaise
1 cup buttermilk

Mix together with wire whip until creamy.
This is excellent on baked potatoes.

CAESAR SALAD DRESSING

1/2 teaspoon salt
1/2 teaspoon dry mustard
1/2 teaspoon garlic powder
1/4 teaspoon black pepper
1/4 teaspoon Worcestershire sauce
1/4 cup lemon juice
1/4 cup oil

Mix together in pint jar and shake until well mixed.
Shake just before pouring over salad.

53

POPPY SEED DRESSING

1¼ cups sugar
2 teaspoons dry mustard
2/3 cup vinegar
1½ teaspoons salt
2 Tablespoons onion juice
2 cups salad or olive oil
3 Tablespoons poppy seeds

Mix sugar, mustard, salt, vinegar and onion juice thoroughly. Slowly add oil, beating constantly until thick. Add poppy seeds and beat a few more minutes. Serve over fruit salad.

THOUSAND ISLAND

1/4 cup chili sauce
1 cup mayonnaise
1/2 teaspoon Worcestershire sauce
2 Tablespoons sweet pickle relish
1 hard-boiled egg, finely diced

Mix together well. Refrigerate.

VINEGAR AND OIL

1 cup olive oil
1/4 cup red wine vinegar
1 teaspoon salt
1 teaspoon white pepper

Mix together and whip until well blended. Any vegetable oil may be substituted for olive oil.

BLUE CHEESE DRESSING

1 cup blue cheese
1¼ cups mayonnaise
1/2 teaspoon pepper
2 Tablespoons lemon juice
1/2 teaspoon Worcestershire sauce
1 Tablespoon chives
1 Tablespoon parsley
1/4 cup cream
dash garlic salt

Crumble blue cheese. Mix with other ingredients and beat until smooth.

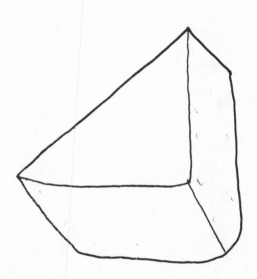

55

OTHER DESIRABLES

Eggs and Cheese

BRUNCH CASSEROLE

6 slices bread, buttered
1½ pounds sausage
1 6-oz package grated cheddar cheese
½ teaspoon dry mustard
1½ teaspoon salt
½ teaspoon pepper
6 eggs
2 cups half and half

Cube bread and cover bottom of 9 inch square pan. Brown, drain, and crumble sausage. Layer sausage, then cheese over bread. Beat remaining ingredients and pour over all. Cover and refrigerate overnight. Bake at 350° for 45 minutes to 1 hour.

DEVILED EGGS

6 eggs, hard-boiled
1 teaspoon prepared mustard
2 teaspoons dill pickle juice
salt and pepper
salad dressing or mayonnaise

Peel eggs, cut in half and separate yolk from white. Mash yolks with fork. Add ingredients in order using enough mayonnaise to make very thick paste. Fill hollows of egg whites.

EGG SALAD

6 eggs, scrambled
2 Tablespoons sweet pickle relish
1 Tablespoon finely chopped onion
1 Tablespoon mustard
mayonnaise

Scramble eggs hard and stir until they break apart in small pieces. Add other ingredients, adding just enough mayonnaise to hold ingredients together. This is a sandwich salad and can be made with mashed boiled eggs.

EGGS BENEDICT WITH CHEESE SAUCE

2 English muffins
4 slices Swiss cheese
4 slices Canadian bacon
4 poached eggs
cheese sauce

Broil muffins until brown. Place 1 bacon slice and 1 cheese slice on each muffin half. Top with poached egg. Pour cheese sauce over all. Serve immediately.

CHEESE SAUCE

1 Tablespoon butter
1 Tablespoon flour
2/3 cup milk
1/2 teaspoon salt
3/4 cup grated cheddar cheese

Melt butter in saucepan slowly. Add flour and blend until smooth. Cook 1 minute stirring constantly. Gradually add milk. Turn heat to medium, stir and cook until thickened. Add cheese and salt and cook until cheese melts.

OMELETTE

2 eggs
1/4 teaspoon salt
sprinkle pepper
1 Tablespoon milk
1 Tablespoon butter

Beat together eggs, salt, pepper, and milk. Melt butter in 6 or 8 inch silverstone skillet. When skillet is hot, pour eggs in and stir until eggs start to set. Pull sides of eggs up and tilt skillet to let egg run under already set part. When egg has set all the way through, fold in half. Cook another minute on each side. Serve immediately. Any desired ingredients may be sprinkled on egg just before folding.

POACHED EGGS

Take a small pan, fill with water, and bring to a boil. Lower heat just enough to still the water and pour egg in from a bowl. Cook until white is firm. Add just a little vinegar to the water and the white will hold it's shape.

BROCCOLI-RICE QUICHE

1/2 cup onions, finely chopped
2 packages frozen chopped broccoli
3 cups hot cooked rice
1 teaspoon salt
1½ cups grated cheddar cheese
6 eggs
1 can sliced mushrooms
1/4 teaspoon pepper
1/2 cup milk

Cook onions with broccoli by package directions. Drain well and set aside. Combine rice, 3/4 cup cheese, 2 eggs and 1/2 teaspoon salt. Press firmly and evenly into two 9 inch pie pans. Beat remaining eggs, stir in milk, pepper, mushrooms, and salt. Add broccoli and pour into crusts. Sprinkle with cheese. Bake 10 minutes. Cool and slice.

SPINACH AND CHEESE QUICHE

1 10-oz. package frozen spinach
1 8-oz. package Swiss cheese slices
2 Tablespoons flour
3 eggs, beaten
1 cup whipping cream
1 teaspoon salt
1/8 teaspoon pepper

Cook spinach and drain well. Cover cheese with flour on both sides and slice in 1 inch strips. Set aside. Combine remaining ingredients, beating well. Stir in spinach and cheese. Pour in baked pastry shell and bake for 1 hour at 350°

QUICHE LORRAINE

10 slices bacon, fried crisp
5 eggs, beaten
2½ cups half and half
1 Tablespoon butter
1 Tablespoon minced onion
1 teaspoon salt
2 teaspoons Worcestershire sauce
1/8 teaspoon nutmeg
1 pound Swiss cheese, grated
3 Tablespoons parmesan cheese

Scatter crumbled bacon over bottom of cooked pie shell. Combine all ingredients except parmesan cheese. Pour into pie shell over bacon and sprinkle top with parmesan cheese. Set on cookie sheet and bake for 20 minutes at 375°. Lower temperature to 350° and bake another 30 minutes.

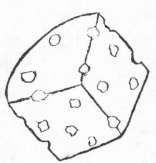

CHEESE BROCCOLI

2 packages frozen broccoli
1/2 pound processed cheese, chopped
1 stick butter
1/2 box round snack crackers, crushed

Boil broccoli in very little water for two minutes only. Drain thoroughly, then stir in cheese and 1/2 butter until both are melted. Put in greased casserole and sprinkle with cracker crumbs and dot with remaining butter. Bake at 350° for 30-35 minutes. Watch closely after 20 minutes.

CHEESE GRITS

1 cup quick cooking grits
1 roll garlic cheese
1 stick butter
2 eggs, beaten
3/4 cup milk
dash cayenne pepper

Cook grits by package directions. Add cheese and butter. Cool. Combine eggs and milk. Put grits in 2 quart casserole dish and pour milk mixture over grits. Bake uncovered for 1 hour at 375°.

CHEESE AND MACARONI

1 8-oz. package macaroni
2½ cups evaporated milk
4 cups American cheese, grated
salt and pepper

Cook macaroni and drain. Add milk and cheese to hot macaroni. Salt and pepper to taste and bake at 300° for 30 minutes.

EASY CHEESY RICE

3 cups hot cooked rice
3/4 cup grated cheddar cheese
1/4 teaspoon salt
1/4 teaspoon pepper
1/2 cup sour cream
1/4 cup bacon bits

Put rice, cheese, salt, and pepper in saucepan and cook slowly until cheese melts. While very hot, stir in sour cream and bacon bits. Serve immediately.

PIMENTO CHEESE

1 pound American cheese, grated
1 jar pimentos, chopped
salt and pepper
mayonnaise

Mix all ingredients using enough mayonnaise to make cheese hold together. Salt and pepper to taste.

CHEESE ENCHILADAS

1 package frozen flour tortillas
1/2 pound cheddar cheese, grated
1/2 pound American cheese, grated
1 large onion, chopped
1 medium can chili, without beans

Turn tortillas in hot grease to make soft. Mix cheese and onion together well, put mixture on tortillas, roll up and place in baking dish. Pour chili over enchiladas and bake at 375° for 45 minutes to 1 hour.

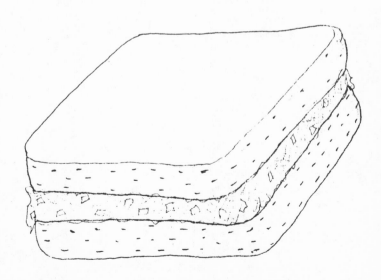

OTHER DESIRABLES

Breads

COUNTRY BISCUITS

2 cups all-purpose flour
1/2 teaspoon salt
1/2 teaspoon soda
3 teaspoons baking powder
2 Tablespoons shortening
1 cup buttermilk
1/4 cup melted butter

Combine dry ingredients. Cut in shortening. Add buttermilk and butter stirring quickly until mixed. Turn out on floured board and knead gently several times. Add more flour if needed. Pat out to 1/2-inch thick and cut with biscuit cutter. Bake 12 to 15 minutes at 400°.

FRIED BISCUITS

1 can small biscuits
butter
jam, jelly, or honey
deep fryer

Open biscuits and separate. Drop individually in very hot oil and cook until brown. Turn and cook on other side until brown. Serve hot with butter and honey, or any jam or jelly you prefer.

GOOD AND EASY BISCUITS

1 cup buttermilk
2 teaspoons oil
dash salt
self-rising flour

Mix buttermilk, oil, and salt. Add flour until dough is thick and you cannot stir with a spoon. Scrap onto floured board and work in flour until dough is no longer sticky. Pull outside edges of dough to middle and turn over. Top side should be smooth. Pat out to about 1/2 to 3/4 inch thick and cut with biscuit cutter. Bake at 425° until brown. Brush top with butter.

EASIEST EVER BANANA NUT BREAD

1 pound cake mix
3 large ripe bananas
1 cup chopped nuts

Mix pound cake by package directions. Mash bananas and stir into cake batter along with nuts. Bake in greased and floured loaf pan per pound cake package directions.

BANANA NUT BREAD

1/2 cup shortening
1 cup sugar
2 eggs
3 bananas, overripe & mashed
1 teaspoon salt
1 teaspoon soda
1 teaspoon baking powder
1 cup chopped nuts
2 cups flour

Cream shortening, sugar, eggs and bananas. Sift dry ingredients and add along with chopped nuts. Bake in greased and floured loaf pan at 350° until toothpick inserted in center comes out clean.

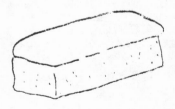

BEER BREAD

3 cups self-rising flour
1 can warm beer
4 Tablespoons sugar

Mix together and pour into greased loaf pan or muffin tins. Bake at 350° for about 1 hour, or until done.

BRAIDED BREAD

3½ cups milk
7 Tablespoons sugar
1 Tablespoon salt
4 Tablespoons oil
4 packages yeast
1 cup warm water
12 cups self-rising flour
1 egg yolk
1/4 cup water
sesame seeds or poppy seeds

Heat milk, sugar, salt and oil to boiling point. Cool. Dissolve yeast in warm water in large greased mixing bowl, then add milk mixture. Add 6 cups flour and mix well, add remaining flour. Make ball out of dough and let rise for 1 hour. Turn out on floured board and knead for 3 minutes. Return to bowl and let rise another hour. Divide the dough into four equal parts. Stretch and shape into long rolls about 1½ inches in diameter. Cut each long roll into three pieces, braid them and tuck ends under. Make four loaves and place on cookie sheet; cover and let rise 1 more hour. Beat egg yolk and water. Brush over loaves and sprinkle with your choice of seeds. Bake at 425° for approximately 20 minutes.

AUNT CILL'S LIGHT BREAD

1 package yeast in 1/2 cup warm water
1½ cups warm water
1 teaspoon salt
2 Tablespoons sugar
2 Tablespoons shortening
flour to make very stiff dough

Combine all ingredients and let rise until double. Punch down and knead well to remove air bubbles. Put in bread pan and let rise until double again. Bake at 450° until golden brown on top.

WHOLE WHEAT BREAD

2 packages yeast
1 teaspoon sugar
3 cups warm water
4 teaspoons salt
3/4 cup brown sugar
4 cups all-purpose flour
1/2 cup butter
1 cup boiling water
8 cups whole wheat flour

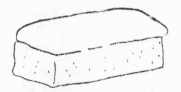

Mix yeast, sugar, and 1/2 cup warm water. Combine $2\frac{1}{2}$ cups warm water, salt, brown sugar, and 2 cups all-purpose flour and mix well. Add to yeast mixture. Cover and set in warm place for $1\frac{1}{2}$ to 2 hours. Melt butter in boiling water, cool. Add whole wheat flour, then stir into yeast mixture. Stir in remaining all-purpose flour. Turn out onto floured board and knead. Place in greased bowl, cover and let rise for 45 minutes. Form loaves, cover and let rise for 30 mintues. Bake at 375° for 35 minutes.

TOFFEE NUT COFFEE CAKE

1 stick butter
2 cups flour
1 cup light brown sugar, packed
1/2 cup granulated sugar
1 cup buttermilk
1 teaspoon baking soda
2 eggs, beaten
1 teaspoon vanilla
6 toffee candy bars
1/2 cup chopped pecans

Mix together butter, flour, and sugars. Divide in half. Take one half and add buttermilk, baking soda, eggs, and vanilla. Mix thoroughly and pour into a greased 9X13 pan. Take crushed toffee candy bars and nuts and mix with other half of butter mixture. Sprinkle over batter in pan. Bake at 350° for 30 minutes.

CINNAMON ROLLS

2¼ cups warm water
1/2 cup shortening
1 egg
1½ teaspoons salt
1/2 cup sugar
2 packages yeast
1/2 cup sugar mixed with 1½ teaspoons cinnamon
melted butter

Dissolve yeast in warm water. Add remaining ingredients to yeast mixture and mix well. Add flour until dough can be taken out and kneaded. Knead well then put back in bowl and let rise until double. Take out and roll flat about 1/2 inch thick. Brush with melted butter then sprinkle with cinnamon and sugar. Roll up and slice. Put in greased pan. When these start to rise, bake at 350°-400° until brown.

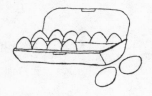

BISCUIT MIX CORNBREAD

1¼ cups biscuit mix
3/4 cup cornmeal
1 Tablespoon sugar
1/2 teaspoon salt
2 eggs
2 Tablespoons shortening
2/3 cup milk

Mix all together. Pour into greased 10-inch iron skillet and bake at 400° until brown.

70

JALAPENO CORNBREAD

1 cup yellow cornmeal
1 cup milk
2 eggs
1 16-oz. can cream style corn
1 pound ground beef, browned and drained
1/2 teaspoon soda
1/2 teaspoon salt
1/2 cup oil
1 pound cheddar cheese, grated
1 onion, finely chopped
2 or 3 jalapeno peppers, minced

Mix meal, milk, eggs, corn, soda, salt and oil. Pour 1/2 of mixture in 9X13 casserole dish, sprinkle with cheese; put beef over cheese then sprinkle onion and pepper. Pour remaining batter over top. Bake at 350° for 50 minutes.

MEXICAN CORNBREAD

1 cup cornmeal
1 cup milk
1/2 teaspoon salt
1½ teaspoons soda, added to milk
1 cup yellow cream style corn
2 eggs
1/2 cup oil
3 jalapeno peppers, minced
1 cup cheddar cheese, grated

Mix all ingredients and bake in large, preheated iron skillet at 400° for 35 to 40 minutes.

QUICK CORNBREAD

1 egg
1½ cups milk
2 Tablespoons melted shortening
1 cup cornmeal
1 cup flour
4 teaspoons baking powder
1 teaspoon salt
1 Tablespoon sugar

Set oven at 400°, melt shortening in pan to be used for baking. Mix and sift dry ingredients into mixing bowl. Add milk and egg, then pour shortening from baking pan into mixture. Beat well and pour into pan. Bake 25 minutes or until brown.

RAY'S CORNBREAD

Put one heaping teaspoon flour in bottom of 1 cup measuring cup. Finish filling with yellow cornmeal. Put in mixing bowl and add 1/4 teaspoon salt, 1/4 teaspoon soda, 1 rounded Tablespoon baking powder, 1/4 teaspoon sugar, 1 egg, and enough buttermilk to reach cornbread consistency. Cover bottom of skillet with oil, get it piping hot, pour in cornbread batter and bake in preheated oven at 450° until golden brown.

EGG NOODLES

2 eggs, beaten
2 Tablespoons water
2 teaspoons salt
all-purpose flour

Mix eggs, water and salt. Add enough flour to make very stiff dough. Divide into 4 equal parts and roll very thin on floured board. Let dry; then cut. This is enough noodles to cook with one boiled hen.

GARLIC AND HONEY FRENCH BREAD

1 loaf French bread
butter
garlic salt
honey

Slice French bread about 1 inch thick. Butter on both sides and sprinkle with garlic salt. Put under broiler until brown then turn and brown other side. Spread with honey.

GINGERBREAD

1/2 cup shortening
1/2 cup sugar
1 cup molasses
1 cup hot water
1 teaspoon soda
1¼ cups flour
1 teaspoon ginger
2 eggs
1/2 teaspoon baking powder
pinch of salt

Cream sugar and shortening. Add molasses and hot water. Sift dry ingredients and add to mixture. Add eggs last. Bake in greased and floured pan at 350° until done.

GINGERBREAD

3 Tablespoons shortening
1/2 cup sugar
1 egg, beaten
1½ cups flour
1/8 teaspoon salt
1 teaspoon ginger
1 teaspoon cinnamon
1 teaspoon soda
1/2 cup buttermilk
1/2 cup molasses

Cream together shortening and sugar. Add egg. Sift dry ingredients and add alternately with buttermilk and syrup. Pour into buttered pan. Bake at 350° for 30 to 45 minutes.

EASIEST EVER MONKEY BREAD

3 cans biscuits
1/2 cup sugar
1 teaspoon cinnamon
melted butter

Open biscuits, separate, and tear into different size pieces. Mix sugar and cinnamon. Shape dough into balls, dip in butter, roll in sugar mixture, and drop into a bundt pan that has been greased and lightly floured. Bake at 400° for 15 minutes or until biscuits have browned.

DOUGHNUTS

3/4 cup milk
1/2 cup sugar
1/2 cup butter
1/4 teaspoon salt
1/4 cup warm water
1 package yeast
1 egg
4 to 4½ cups flour
deep oil to fry

Combine milk, sugar, butter, and salt. Heat until butter is melted and bubbles start to appear around edges of pan. Cool to lukewarm. Put warm water in large mixing bowl and dissolve yeast. Add milk mixture and egg. Add flour 2 cups at a time. Turn dough out on floured board and knead 7 minutes or until dough is smooth. Place in greased bowl, grease top, cover and let rise until double. Punch down to remove air. Let rest 10 minutes. Roll out to 1/4 inch and cut with doughnut cutter. Let rise until doubled in size. Fry in very hot oil until brown, turn over and brown. Sift lightly with powdered sugar, or dip in glaze made with powdered sugar and milk or water.

EASIEST EVER DONUTS

1 can biscuits
oil
powdered sugar
water

Open biscuits and separate. Cut center out with any small bottle or bottle top. Drop in very hot deep oil and fry until brown, turn and brown. Mix powdered sugar and water to make a thin glaze. Pour over donuts.

HUSH PUPPIES

1½ cups cornmeal
1/2 cup flour
2 Tablespoons baking powder
1 teaspoon salt
2/3 cup yellow cream style corn
1/2 cup minced onion
1 egg
1/2 cup buttermilk
3 Tablespoons oil

Mix together and drop by teaspoon in deep hot oil. Fry until brown, turn and brown other side.

SOUTHERN HUSH PUPPIES

2 cups cornmeal
1 cup buttermilk
1/2 teaspoon baking powder
1 teaspoon salt
1 egg
1/2 cup finely chopped onion

Thoroughly mix all ingredients. Drop by tablespoon into hot deep fat and fry until golden brown.

HUSH PUPPIES

1½ cups cornmeal mix
1/2 cup flour
2 Tablespoons baking powder
2 Tablespoons sugar
1/2 teaspoon salt
1/2 cup chopped onion
1 egg
milk

Mix all ingredients adding milk last. Use just enough milk to make stiff, gooey batter. Drop by spoon into hot deep oil.

BASIC MUFFIN

2 cups flour
1/2 teaspoon salt
3 teaspoons baking powder
3/4 cup sugar
2 eggs
1 cup milk
1/4 cup melted butter

Mix dry ingredients and set aside. Combine eggs, milk and butter, and pour into dry ingredients. Stir only enough to moisten.   (Batter will be lumpy) Fill muffin cups 2/3 full and bake at 400° about 15 minutes.   Blueberries, cherries, bananas, nuts, etc. can be added to this basic muffin recipe.

OATMEAL MUFFINS

1 cup sifted all-purpose flour
1/4 cup sugar
3 teaspoons baking powder
1/2 teaspoon salt
1 cup quick-cooking oats
1 beaten egg
1 cup milk
3 Tablespoons oil

Sift dry ingredients. Mix egg, milk, and oil and add to dry ingredients, adding oats last and stirring just enough to moisten. Fill greased muffin pan 2/3 full and bake at 425° for 15 minutes.

PANCAKES

1 cup milk
1 egg, beaten
2 Tablespoons oil
Pinch of salt
1 teaspoon baking powder

Add flour until you have the desired consistency. The thinner the batter, the thinner the pancake. Pour on hot buttered griddle and cook until batter starts to dry, turn and brown on other side.

PLAIN PANCAKES

2 cups sifted flour
6 teaspoons baking powder
1/4 cup sugar
1 teaspoon salt
2 eggs
2 cups milk
1/3 cup oil

Sift together flour, sugar, baking powder and salt. Beat eggs and stir in milk and oil. Add dry ingredients and beat to a smooth batter. Pour onto hot griddle and cook until bubbles come through and batter starts to look dry, turn and brown on other side.

WEDNESDAY NIGHT PANCAKES

2½ cups buttermilk
1 cup all-purpose flour
1 cup self-rising flour
2 teaspoons baking powder
3 eggs, beaten

Mix together adding more or less milk for desired consistency. Cook on hot buttered griddle.

PIZZA CRUST

1 package yeast
1 cup warm water
1 teaspoon sugar
1/2 teaspoon salt
2 Tablespoons oil
2 to 2½ cups flour

Dissolve yeast in water. Add remaining ingredients in order. Mix well. Let set for 10 minutes. Roll out dough and put on pizza pan. Top with your favorite pizza topping. Bake for 30 minutes at 425°.

MAMA'S JELLY ROLL

2 egg yolks, beaten (save whites)
1 cup sugar
3 Tablespoons water
1 cup flour
1½ teaspoons baking powder
1/2 teaspoon salt

Beat yolks and add sugar. Slowly add water, flour, baking powder, and salt beating after each ingredient. Beat egg whites until stiff and fold into mixture. Spread thin on a well greased and floured sheet pan. Bake at 350° for about 15 minutes. Turn out on damp cloth, spread with jelly and roll while hot. Chocolate sauce may be used instead of jelly.

EASY NO-KNEAD ROLLS

2 to 2½ cups warm water
1 package yeast
3 Tablespoons sugar
2 teaspoons salt
4 Tablespoons cooking oil
5 to 6 cups flour

Dissolve yeast in warm water. Add sugar, salt and oil. Stir in as much flour as possible with spoon. Grease muffin tins and fill each tin with a spoonful of dough and let rise till double. Bake at 425° until brown.

LIGHT ROLLS

2 packages yeast
2 cups very warm water
1 egg
1/4 cup shortening
1 teaspoon salt
1/2 cup sugar
6 to 7 cups flour

Dissolve yeast in warm water. Cream together egg and shortening, then mix with 3 cups of flour and yeast mixture. Add remaining ingredients, turn out on lightly floured board and knead well. Refrigerate overnight covered with damp cloth. Pinch off as needed, put in muffin tins and let rise. Bake at 400° until brown.

NONA'S LIGHT ROLLS

1/2 cup warm water
1 package yeast
6 Tablespoons sugar
3 Tablespoons oil
1½ cups warm water
1 teaspoon salt
6 cups flour (approximately)

Mix together 1/2 cup water, yeast, sugar and oil. Let set for 5 minutes. Add other ingredients and knead well. Let rise until double. Punch down to remove air pockets. Pinch off rolls, put in pan and let rise again. Bake at 350° until brown.

PERFECT REFRIGERATOR ROLLS

1 cup boiling water
2 sticks butter
3/4 cup sugar
1/2 teaspoon salt
3 packages yeast
1 cup warm water
1 teaspoon sugar
2 eggs, beaten
6 cups flour

In large bowl mix together boiling water, butter, sugar, and salt. Set aside and let cool. Dissolve yeast in warm water and 1 teaspoon sugar. Mix these two together with eggs. Beat in flour last. Let rise in refrigerator covered overnight. Shape into rolls and let rise till double. Bake at 425° until done.

QUICK ROLLS

1 package yeast
1 cup lukewarm water
1 teaspoon sugar
1/2 cup warm milk
1 teaspoon salt
3 Tablespoons sugar
1 egg, beaten
3 Tablespoons shortening, melted
3 cups flour, more or less as needed

Dissolve yeast and 1 teaspoon sugar with water. Mix together warm milk, salt, sugar, and beaten egg. Add shortening, and yeast mixture. Mix in flour until dough is no longer sticky. Let rise until double in bulk at room temperature. Turn onto floured board and work. Shape into rolls or loaves, place in greased pan and let rise until double again. Bake 10-15 minutes at 350°.

RITA'S REFRIGERATOR ROLLS

1 package dry yeast (dissolved in 1/4 cup warm water)
1 stick oleo (melted)
2 eggs, beaten
1/2 cup sugar
5 cups self-rising flour
2 cups buttermilk

Combine oleo, buttermilk and sugar. Beat just a little. When cool, add beaten eggs and yeast mixture. Add flour, mix well and place in covered bowl in refrigerator. This will keep for several days. To bake as needed, roll out and cut as you would biscuits. Place in greased pan with butter on top of rolls. Bake at 400° for approximately 20 minutes.

FRENCH TOAST

2 eggs
1/2 cup milk
1/2 teaspoon salt
bread slices

Mix together, dip bread slices in mixture turning to coat both sides. Fry in small amount of oil or butter until both sides are browned.

FRENCH TOAST

2 eggs, slightly beaten
3/4 cup milk
1/4 teaspoon salt
2 teaspoons sugar
8 slices bread
3 to 4 Tablespoons oil for frying

Combine eggs, milk, salt, and sugar. Heat 2 tablespoons oil in frying pan. Dip bread, one slice at a time in egg mixture. Fry over low heat. Flip when first side browns and brown other side. Add oil as needed. Serve with jelly, syrup, etc. Good sprinkled with powdered sugar.

OTHER DESIRABLES

Meats

and

Casseroles

AMERICAN FRIED RICE

1 pound ground beef, browned and drained
3 slices bacon, fried and crumbled
1 large bell pepper, chopped
1/2 cup onion, chopped
2 eggs, scrambled
3 cups cooked rice

Saute onion and pepper in bacon drippings until tender. Mix all ingredients together with rice.

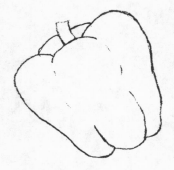

BOUNTY RICE

1 pound ground beef
1 can tomatoes
1/2 teaspoon garlic powder
4 cups shredded cabbage
1 cup Monterey Jack cheese
1 cup onions
1/2 cup bell pepper
1 Tablespoon salt
1 Tablespoon chili powder
3 cups cooked rice
1/2 cup sour cream

Brown meat with onion and bell pepper. Drain and stir in tomatoes, seasonings, rice and cabbage. Cover and cook 10 to 15 minutes or until cabbage is tender-crisp. Stir in sour cream. Sprinkle with grated cheese. Cover and cook until cheese melts.

CABBAGE ROLLS

1 pound ground beef
1 onion, chopped
1/2 cup mayonnaise
1 egg
salt, pepper, garlic salt, and Worcestershire sauce to taste

Mix all of the above ingredients together well. Remove core from whole cabbage head. Put in 1" water and cook for 25 minutes over low heat. Pull leaves off, put meat mixture in cabbage leaves and fold over. Put unused cabbage in bottom of pan, lay stuffed leaves on top and pour catsup over all. Bake at 300° for 2 hours covered.

ENCHILADA CASSEROLE

2 pounds ground chuck
1 large diced onion
1 can cream of mushroom soup
1 can cream of chicken soup
1 can enchilada sauce
1 can soft tortillas
1 8-oz. block cheddar cheese, grated

Brown ground chuck and onion. Drain, add soups and enchilada sauce and simmer for 15 minutes. Layer in a 9X13 pan 1/2 tortillas, 1/2 sauce and 1/2 grated cheese - repeat layers. Bake at 350° for 30 minutes.

GROUND BEEF AND NOODLES

1 12-oz. package noodles
1½ pounds ground beef
1 large onion, chopped
1 bell pepper, chopped
1 stalk celery, chopped
2 cans tomato soup
2 cans cream of mushroom soup
1 pound cheddar cheese, grated

Cook noodles and drain. Brown ground beef with onions, peppers, and celery. Simmer soups and cheese until cheese melts. Stir all together and put in greased baking dish and bake at 325° for 30 minutes.

HAMBURGER AND NOODLE BAKE

1½ pounds ground chuck
2 8-oz. cans tomato sauce
1 medium package noodles, cooked
1 cup sour cream
1 8-oz. package cream cheese, cubed
1 bunch green onions, chopped
garlic, salt and pepper to taste
1 8-oz. package cheddar cheese

Brown meat with seasonings. Add tomato sauce and simmer for 15 minutes. Mix cream cheese, sour cream and onions. Layer noodles, meat mixture, and sour cream mixture and top with grated cheddar cheese. Bake at 300° until cheese melts.

HAMBURGERS

1 pound ground beef
1/2 cup quick cooking oats
1/2 cup tomato juice
1 teaspoon salt
1 onion
mustard or pickle relish
oil

Put ground beef, oats, and tomato juice in mixing bowl. Add salt and a little pepper and mix well. Shape into 6 patties. Fry in very little oil until brown on both sides. Serve with onion, mustard, and pickle relish.

ITALIAN BEEF

1½ pounds ground beef
1 teaspoon salt
1/2 cup chopped onion
1 teaspoon minced garlic
1 teaspoon oregano
1 can tomato soup
1/2 cup water
2 cups cooked noodles
1 cup shredded cheese

Brown meat with onions, garlic and oregano. Drain and add cooked noodles. Add water, tomato soup, salt and put in baking dish. Top with cheese and bake at 400° until cheese melts.

LASAGNE

1½ pounds ground beef
2 pounds canned tomatoes
1 8-oz. can seasoned tomato sauce
1 package spaghetti sauce mix
2 cloves garlic, crushed
1 8-oz. package lasagne noodles
1 8-oz. package American cheese, grated
1 cup parmesan cheese
1 cup cream style cottage cheese

Brown meat and spoon off excess fat. Add tomatoes, sauce, sauce mix, and garlic. Cover and simmer for 45 minutes stirring occasionally. Cook noodles until tender. In long baking dish, place 1/2 of the cooked noodles in bottom. Cover with 1/3 of the sauce mix, 1/2 American cheese and 1/2 cottage cheese. Repeat layering and put final 1/3 of sauce last and top with parmesan cheese. Bake for 30 minutes at 350°. Let stand 10 to 15 minutes before serving.

MEAT LOAF

1 pound ground beef
1/4 pound sausage
2 Tablespoons melted butter
1 egg, slightly beaten
2 Tablespoons chopped onions
1/4 teaspoon pepper
1 cup milk
1 cup coarsely broken crackers
1 teaspoon salt

Combine all ingredients. Form into loaf and lay 2 or 3 slices of bacon on top. Bake at 375° for 2 hours.

POTATO GOULASH

2 pounds ground beef
1 large onion, chopped
1 small can English peas
1 Tablespoon butter
1 Tablespoon cornstarch
8 medium potatoes

Saute onions in butter for 5 minutes. Add meat and brown. Add peas and thicken with corn starch in a little water. Peel potatoes and dice into 1/4-inch cubes and country fry until tender. Mix all together and simmer covered for 15 mintues.

RED BEANS AND RICE

1 pound ground beef
1 large onion, chopped
1 large bell pepper, chopped
1 Tablespoon chili powder
2 teaspoons salt
1 16-oz. can tomatoes or juice
1 cup water
1½ cups uncooked rice
1 can red kidney beans

Brown meat with onions and peppers. Add remaining ingredients and simmer for 15 minutes. Remove from heat and pour into 9X13 pan. Evenly distribute 1½ cups uncooked rice and 1 can red kidney beans in mixture. Cover and bake at 350° for 1 hour. Take out and stir, cover and return to oven for another 15 minutes.

SLOPPY JOES

1 pound ground beef, browned and drained
1 can chicken gumbo soup
1/4 cup chopped celery
1/8 teaspoon dry mustard
2 Tablespoons catsup

Mix well and simmer 10 minutes. Serve over buns.

SPANISH RICE

1 pound ground beef
1 small onion, chopped
1 bell pepper, chopped
1-1/3 cups raw rice
2 cups hot water
1 teaspoon salt
1/4 teaspoon pepper
1 teaspoon chili powder
2 cans tomato sauce

Cook onion, pepper, ground beef and rice until lightly browned. Stir in remaining ingredients and bring to a boil. Lower heat and simmer covered till rice is tender. Approximately 40 minutes.

STUFFED BELL PEPPERS

1 pound ground beef
1 medium onion, chopped
1 teaspoon sugar
1/2 teaspoon rubbed sage
1/2 teaspoon parsley flakes
1 teaspoon salt
3 Tablespoons butter
1½ cups cooked rice
2 cans tomato sauce
6 medium size bell peppers

Saute onion in butter until tender. Add ground beef, parsley flakes and sugar and brown lightly. Add all the other ingredients. Core and remove seeds from bell peppers. Pour boiling water over and let set for 5 minutes. Drain and fill with meat mixture. Place in shallow pan and put any remaining meat mixture evenly around peppers. Top each pepper with catsup, cover and bake for 30 minutes at 350°. Uncover and cook another 15 minutes until brown. Parmesan cheese can be sprinkled on top when uncovered before cooking last 15 minutes.

STUFFED BISCUITS

1 pound ground beef
1/2 cup barbeque sauce
1 small onion, chopped
2 Tablespoons brown sugar
1 8-oz. can biscuits
3/4 cup grated cheese

Mash biscuits in muffin pan to form crust. Brown beef
and onion. Add sauce and brown sugar and simmer for
10 minutes. Put mixture in biscuit and top with
cheese. Bake at 400° until biscuits are done and
cheese melted.

TACOS

1 pound ground beef
1 8-oz. can tomato sauce
1 pint pinto beans
1/2 teaspoon chili powder
lettuce
grated cheese
fresh tomato, chopped

Brown meat and drain. Add tomato sauce, beans and
chili powder. Simmer until most of liquid is gone.
Place meat mixture in taco shells. Top with lettuce,
cheese and chopped fresh tomatoes.

TORTILLA WONDER

1 pound ground beef
1 onion, chopped
1 clove garlic, minced
1 16-oz. can tomato sauce
1/2 cup sliced black olives
1½ Tablespoons chili powder
1/2 teaspoon salt
6 large corn tortillas
2 cups cheddar cheese, grated

Brown meat, onion and garlic. Drain off fat and add
tomato sauce, olives, chili powder, salt. Simmer
about 5 minutes. In 9-inch pan, layer small amount of
meat sauce, cheese, then tortilla. Repeat until all
ingredients are used. Top with cheese, cover and bake
at 400° for 25 minutes. Remove foil and let stand 5
to 10 minutes before cutting into four wedges.

BEEF STROGANOFF

1 pound cubed round steak
1 Tablespoon dry mustard
3 Tablespoons flour
1 teaspoon salt
1/2 teaspoon pepper
1/4 pound butter
1 large onion
1 can sliced mushrooms
1 can tomato soup
1/2 can water
1 8-oz. carton sour cream

Put steak cubes in bowl. Sift dry ingredients over
meat and mix well. Let set 1/2 hour. Fry in 1/2 of
butter over high heat until browned. Thinly slice
onions and saute along with mushrooms in other half of
butter. In large skillet, mix steak, onions and
remaining ingredients, except sour cream, and simmer
for 2 hours. Add sour cream after taking off stove.
Serve over noodles or rice.

BEEF BRISKET

2 Tablespoons liquid smoke
2 teaspoons celery seed
1 Tablespoon Worcestershire sauce
1 teaspoon garlic salt
3 Tablespoons soy sauce
1 teaspoon pepper
1½ teaspoons salt
1 4-pound brisket

Combine first seven ingredients. Put brisket in aluminum foil, fat side up and pour marinade over. Seal foil tightly and let set in refrigerator overnight. Bake in foil 5½ hours at 275°.

BEEF TERIYAKI

2 pounds sirloin steak
1¼ cups soy sauce
1/2 cup sugar
1/8 teaspoon dry minced garlic
1 teaspoon ground ginger
2 Tablespoons sherry

Lightly salt and pepper steak and set aside. Mix all other ingredients together and marinate steak for 1 hour. Broil steak until done.

CAL'S ROUND STEAK

1 whole untenderized round steak
1 onion, thinly sliced
2 packages brown gravy mix
4 bay leaves
pepper and flour

Pepper and flour steak. Mix both gravy packages by only one package recipe. Place 1/2 onion in bottom of electric skillet with 1/3 gravy and 2 bay leaves. Place round steak over this and top with the remaining onions, gravy and bay leaves. Cover and simmer for 4½ hours. Cook on very low heat.

93

PEPPER STEAK

1 whole round steak
1/4 cup oil
1/8 teaspoon dry minced garlic
1 teaspoon salt
1 teaspoon ground ginger
1/2 teaspoon pepper
4 large bell peppers, sliced in strips
2 large onions, thinly sliced
1/2 cup soy sauce
3/4 cup beef bouillon
1 6-oz. can sliced water chestnuts
2 Tablespoons cornstarch
1/2 cup water

Slice steak into 1/8th-inch wide strips. Heat oil in skillet, add garlic, salt, ginger and pepper. Saute for 5 minutes, add steak slices and brown lightly. Remove and put peppers and onions in skillet and cook for 4 minutes. Put beef in skillet with other ingredients. Add soy sauce, bouillon, water chestnuts and cornstarch dissolved in water. Simmer about 4 minutes or until sauce thickens.

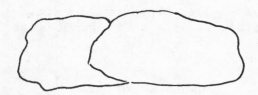

ROAST BEEF HASH

2 cups chopped leftover roast
left over roast gravy
4 potatoes, cubed
1 large onion, chopped
cornstarch to thicken

Place all ingredients in large saucepan. Simmer until potatoes and onions are tender. Water, beef broth, and cornstarch can be added as needed for liquid.

POT ROAST

1 4 to 6 pound chuck roast
4 Tablespoons oil
1 package onion soup mix
3 large onions, quartered
1 medium cabbage, quartered
1 package carrots, halved
6 medium potatoes, halved
salt and pepper

Salt and pepper roast and brown in skillet with oil. Put in large roasting pan with water to 3/4 cover roast. Add onion soup mix and cook covered on low to medium heat until meat is tender (approximately 3 to 4 hours). Add water during cooking if necessary. When meat is tender, add vegetables and cook covered until done. Remove vegetables and meat from pan and arrange on platter with roast in the middle and vegetables placed around. Use cornstarch mixed with a little water to thicken broth. Be sure broth is boiling when you pour in cornstarch.

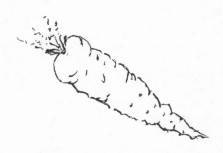

SWISS STEAK

4 minute steaks, tenderized
1 chopped onion
1 10-oz. can whole tomatoes
flour
salt and pepper

Salt, pepper and flour both sides of steak and brown in oil with the chopped onion. Add tomatoes, cover, lower heat and simmer approximately 35 to 45 minutes.

CORNED BEEF AND CABBAGE

1 medium size cabbage head, chopped
4 carrots, sliced
4 medium potatoes, quartered
1 onion, chopped
1 can corned beef
salt and pepper to taste

In a large saucepan, boil the carrots with enough water to cover. Add the potatoes after the carrots are half done. Boil together approximately 5 minutes and add chopped cabbage and onion. When the cabbage is cooked, add the corned beef. Mix well and season to taste. If too juicy, stir in 3 or 4 Tablespoons instant mashed potatoes to thicken.

SMOTHERED LIVER

4 to 6 pieces calf liver
1 large onion, thinly sliced
1 beef bouillon cube
flour
salt and pepper

Salt, pepper and flour liver. Brown in skillet with onions until liver is done. Dissolve bouillon cube in 1½ cups boiling water and pour over liver. Cover and simmer for 30 to 45 minutes. Stir often. Thicken with cornstarch mixed with a small amount of water if this does not thicken itself.

BREADED VEAL CUTLETS

2 Tablespoons butter
1 egg, beaten
2 Tablespoons milk
1 teaspoon salt
4 veal cutlets
1 cup fine cracker crumbs

Combine egg, milk and salt. Dip veal in egg mixture and roll in crumbs. Place in skillet with melted butter and brown for 10 minutes on each side. Cook cutlets until tender.

96

VEAL PARMESAN

1/4 cup flour
1/2 teaspoon salt
pepper to taste
2 Tablespoons butter
2/3 cup evaporated milk
3/4 cup grated parmesan cheese
4 pieces veal
1 8-oz. can tomato sauce

Combine 1/4 cup parmesan cheese, flour, salt and pepper. Dip veal in 1/2 of the milk and then the cheese and flour mixture. Place in 9-inch square pan in which the butter has been melted. Bake for 30 minutes at 350°. Mix remaining milk and parmesan cheese. Spread tomato sauce over veal and sprinkle cheese mixture on top. Bake for 20 more minutes.

SWEET AND SOUR PORK

2 pounds pork, cut in pieces
1 large bell pepper
2 stalks celery, chopped
1 large onion, chopped
1/2 cup soy sauce
1/4 cup vinegar
1/4 cup sugar
2 Tablespoons lemon juice
1 clove garlic, pressed
1 cup water
flour
oil

Flour meat and brown. Put meat in 3 quart casserole and keep warm. In skillet where meat browned, saute onions until clear, add other vegetables and cook 5 minutes. Combine water, vinegar, soy sauce, sugar, and lemon juice. Put 1 Tablespoon flour in 1/4-cup water and add to the liquid. Pour in skillet with vegetables and cook until sauce thickens. Add meat to mixture and let simmer for 5 minutes. Serve over white or fried rice.

BAKED PORK CHOPS

4 to 6 pork chops
salt and pepper
1 can golden mushroom soup
1 onion, thinly sliced
2 Tablespoons butter

Saute onion rings in butter until clear and tender crisp. Salt and pepper pork chops and brown in skillet. Place pork chops in casserole pour soup over and top with onions. Bake at 350° for 30 minutes.

PORK CHOPS IN CHEESE SAUCE

4 pork chops
salt and pepper
1 can cheddar cheese soup
1/2 can milk

Salt and pepper pork chops and brown. When pork chops are done, mix soup and milk and pour over pork chops. Cover and simmer for 15 minutes stirring often.

WILD RICE AND PORK CHOPS

1 box wild rice
6 pork chops
3 Tablespoons oil
1/4 cup slivered almonds
1/2 cup mushrooms, sliced
1/2 cup bell pepper, chopped
1/2 cup onion, chopped
4 Tablespoons butter
1 can cream of mushroom soup

Prepare rice by package directions and add soup. Saute almonds, mushrooms, pepper and onions in butter and add to rice. Salt and pepper pork chops and brown in oil until almost done. Put rice mixture in baking dish, lay pork chops on top and bake uncovered for 30 minutes at 350°.

BUDDY'S RED BEANS AND RICE

2 large onions, finely chopped
2 stalks celery, finely chopped
1/2 bell pepper, finely chopped
4 cloves garlic, finely chopped
2 Tablespoons vegetable oil
4 Tablespoons Worcestershire sauce
1 teaspoon hot sauce
4 bay leaves
2 teaspoons salt
crushed red pepper to taste
1 small can tomato paste
1 ham hock
5 cans red kidney beans

Saute first four ingredients in oil in large pot approximately 15 minutes or until onion is transparent. Add remaining ingredients and simmer approximately 3 hours, stirring occasionally. Serve over white rice.

HAM AND CHEESE MACARONI

1 package elbow macaroni, cooked
1 cup diced ham
1 cup grated cheddar cheese
2 Tablespoons butter
2 Tablespoons flour
3 cups milk
1 teaspoon salt
1/4 teaspoon pepper
1 cup grated American cheese

Mix together butter, flour, milk, salt and pepper. Cook until blended and thickened, stirring constantly. Add grated American cheese. Put macaroni in casserole dish, pour sauce over and add ham and cheddar cheese. Bake at 350° until cheese melts.

SNUGGLED WIENERS AND CHEESE

4 wieners
4 slices bacon
4 slices cheese
mustard or chili sauce
hot dog buns

Preheat oven to 350°. Slit each wiener to make a pocket. Put slice of cheese in each wiener, wrap bacon around and fasten ends with toothpicks. Place in baking dish and bake for 15 minutes. Serve on buns with mustard or chili sauce.

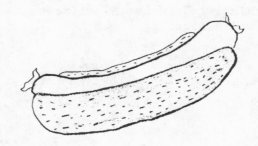

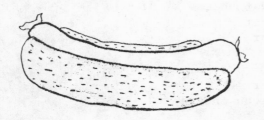

OTHER DESIRABLES

OTHER DESIRABLES

Poultry

BAKED CHICKEN BREASTS

6 chicken breasts
1 can cream of chicken soup
1 small carton sour cream
1 can sliced mushrooms with liquid
1/2 cup sherry wine

Put chicken in shallow baking dish. Mix all other ingredients and pour over chicken. Sprinkle salt, pepper, and paprika on top and bake covered for 30 minutes, then uncovered for 1 hour at 350°. Baste several times with juice around chicken.

CHICKEN AMANDINE

1/2 cup bell pepper, chopped
4 Tablespoons butter
1/3 cup flour
2 cups chicken broth
1 cup half and half
1 teaspoon salt
4 cups diced cooked chicken
1 can sliced mushrooms
3 Tablespoons cooking sherry
1 small jar pimentos, diced
1/2 cup toasted chopped almonds
pepper

Saute bell pepper in butter. Blend in flour and add broth and half and half. Add salt, pepper, chicken and mushrooms. Simmer for 30 minutes. Add remaining ingredients just before serving and serve on toast.

CHICKEN CASSEROLE

1½ cups mayonnaise
1 cup celery, chopped
1 can cream of chicken soup
1 can cream of mushroom or celery soup
3 cups chopped cooked chicken
6 hard-boiled eggs, chopped
1 small jar pimentos
1 cup chicken broth
1/2 cup milk
3 cups cooked rice or noodles
1/2 pound processed cheese, cubed
potato chips

Mix all ingredients together, except potato chips, and bake 1 hour at 350°. After 45 minutes, remove from oven and top with crushed potato chips. This can be frozen and then baked.

CHICKEN AND EGG NOODLES

1 chicken
1/4 cup butter
1 large onion, chopped
2 stalks celery, chopped
3 eggs
salt and pepper
flour

Place chicken, butter, onion and celery in pot, cover with water and boil until tender. When tender, remove from heat, let cool and debone. Put chicken meat back in broth. Beat eggs well, salt and pepper to taste and add enough flour to make a dough. Roll out on floured board and cut noodles. Do not let dry. Drop into boiling broth while dough is still wet. Cook until tender.

105

CHICKEN KIEV

8 split chicken breasts
salt
1/3 cup green onions, chopped
1 Tablespoon parsley flakes
1 stick butter
flour
1 egg
seasoned bread crumbs

Skin breasts and cut away bone. Place between two
pieces of plastic wrap and pound chicken to 1/4-inch
thick. Salt breasts and sprinkle each with 1/2
Tablespoon onion and parsley. Dab with butter and
roll each piece, folding in sides tightly to seal.
Dust chicken with flour, dip in beaten egg, and roll
in bread crumbs. Chill thoroughly then fry in deep
fat at 340° for 5 to 7 minutes or until golden brown.

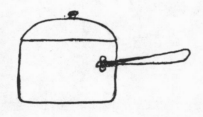

CHICKEN PARMESAN

8 fryer breasts
1 stick butter, melted
16 crackers, crushed
4 Tablespoons parmesan cheese
1 teaspoon paprika
salt and pepper

Mix together cracker crumbs, cheese and paprika. Salt
and pepper chicken, dip in melted butter then in
cracker and cheese mix. Place in buttered casserole.
Pour remaining cracker mix on top and bake 1¼ hours in
350° oven.

CHICKEN SPAGHETTI

1 cup celery, finely chopped
1/2 cup bell pepper, finely chopped
3/4 cup onion, finely chopped
1/2 cup butter
1 can cream of mushroom soup
1 cup chicken broth
2 cups boiled chicken, chunked
1/2 pound spaghetti, cooked
1/2 pound cheddar cheese, grated

Saute celery, onion and bell pepper in butter until tender. Add soup and chicken broth. Salt and pepper to taste. Mix chicken with drained spaghetti and soup mixture. Put in a 9X13 casserole, top with cheese and bake at 350° for 30 minutes.

CHICKEN TETRAZZINI

2 chickens
1 bell pepper, chopped
1 onion, chopped
1 Tablespoon flour
1 large package noodles
1 can cream of mushroom soup
1 can pimento, diced
1 roll garlic cheese, grated
1/2 pound cheddar cheese, grated
1 egg, beaten
3 Tablespoons dry milk

Boil chickens, pull from bone and cut into pieces. Cook onion and pepper in butter until tender, add flour and set aside. Cook noodles in broth from chicken. In separate pan combine soup, pimento, cheese and egg. Cook until cheese melts, add dry milk and salt to taste. Mix all together and bake in large casserole dish for 45 minutes at 350°.

CITY SLICKER CHICKEN

8 chicken breasts, skinned and boned
1/2 cup oil
1 cup flour, salted and peppered
1 large onion, chopped
2 large bell peppers, chopped
1/8 teaspoon minced garlic
3 teaspoons curry powder
1/2 teaspoon pepper
2 teaspoons salt
1/2 teaspoon thyme
2 cans tomatoes
1 teaspoon parsley flakes
2 cups rice
5 cups chicken broth

Flour chicken and fry in oil until browned. Keep warm while sauteing onions, peppers, and garlic in oil where chicken cooked. Add remaining ingredients, except chicken, cook and stir for 8 minutes. Put chicken in casserole dish and pour sauce over. Bake at 350° for 40 minutes. Cook rice in chicken broth. When all liquid has cooked from rice, cover and let steam for 30 minutes. Put rice on large platter, making a hole in center. Place chicken in hole with rice heaped around sides. Pour sauce over rice.

HOT CHICKEN SALAD

2 cups diced cooked chicken
1 cup mayonnaise
2 Tablespoons minced onion
1/2 cup diced celery
1 Tablespoon lemon juice
1 cup cooked rice
1/2 cup slivered almonds
1 can cream of chicken soup
1 egg, beaten
crackers

Mix all ingredients, put in buttered casserole and crumble crackers on top. Bake at 350° for 30 minutes.

DOROTHY'S CHICKEN CASSEROLE

1 large chicken, boiled and boned
1 large onion, chopped
½ cup celery, chopped
1 can cream of mushroom soup
1 can English peas
1 jar sliced mushrooms
1 bell pepper, chopped
2 eggs, hard-boiled and chopped
1 large package egg noodles
1 pound cheddar cheese, grated

Cook chicken with onion and celery. Remove chicken from broth and add mushroom soup and noodles. Cook until noodles are done. Add other ingredients and put in large casserole dish. Cover top with cheese. Bake at 350° until cheese melts and broth bubbles through.

EASY CHICKEN AND RICE

1 onion, chopped
1 13-oz. can chicken broth
1 can boned chicken
1 cup processed cheese, grated
1/2 cup uncooked rice

Mix all ingredients together and bake covered for 1 hour at 375°.

NO PEEK CHICKEN CASSEROLE

1 fryer, cut up
3 cups cooked white rice
1 cup milk
1 can celery soup
1 can mushroom soup
1 package onion soup mix

Layer rice in bottom of large buttered casserole. Heat milk and soups and pour over rice. Lay cut up chicken on top and sprinkle onion soup mix over all. Bake covered at 350° for 2¼ hours.

THE ORIGINAL SOUTHERN FRIED CHICKEN

1 chicken, cut up
salt and pepper
flour
oil

Wash chicken. While wet, salt and pepper to taste. Dip in flour and coat on both sides. Put in skillet with about 1-inch deep oil. Fry fast until brown and crisp on both sides, lower heat and cook until tender, turning if necessary.

CORNISH HEN

2 cornish hens
salt, pepper, garlic salt to taste
4 Tablespoons butter
3/4 cup onion, chopped
1/4 cup celery, chopped

Season hens. Rub outside with butter. Place inside each hen: 1 Tablespoon butter, half of the onion and half of the celery. Bake at 350° until tender and brown.

ROAST GOOSE

3/4 cup onion, chopped
1/4 cup butter
4 cups dry bread crumbs
water
1½ teaspoons salt
1/2 teaspoon pepper
2 eggs
1 can kraut
1 8 to 10 pound goose

Saute onion in butter and mix with bread, salt, pepper, eggs and kraut. Stuff goose with this mixture and place in roasting pan, breast down, in approximately 4 inches water. Bake covered for 1½ hours at 350°. Drain all but 2 inches of water and bake uncovered for 2 hours. Baste occasionally.

OTHER DESIRABLES

OTHER DESIRABLES

Seafood and Fish

BAKED FISH

2 pounds fish fillets
3/4 cup milk
salt and pepper
butter

Put fillets in baking dish. Pour milk over and dot with butter. Salt and pepper to taste. Bake at 375° for 25 minutes.

BROILED HALIBUT OR FLOUNDER

1 egg
1/2 cup milk
6 slices fish
1/2 cup flour
1/2 cup cornmeal
12 crackers, crumbled
salt, pepper, and paprika to taste

Mix egg and milk. Mix flour and cornmeal. Dip fish in egg mixture and roll in flour mixture. Dip in egg mixture, then in cracker crumbs. Put in casserole, season, and dot with butter. Bake at 375° for 20 minutes. Broil for 1 minute. Serve with lemons or lemon juice.

CRAWFISH ETOUFEE

1 pound peeled crawfish tails
1 cup white onions, finely chopped
3/4 cup celery, finely chopped
1 bunch green onions, finely chopped
1/3 cup parsley, chopped
1 stick butter
1 Tablespoon seafood seasoning

Cook white onion and celery in butter until clear. Add green onions and parsley, cook 10 minutes more, and add seafood seasoning. Add crawfish and cook 10 minutes, or until the tails curl. Serve over hot rice.

114

CRAB AU GRATIN

1 cup crab meat
1 cup mayonnaise
1 teaspoon horseradish
1 cup grated cheddar cheese

Mix all ingredients except cheese. Spread in casserole dish and top with cheese. Bake at 450° for 10 minutes or until hot and cheese melts.

CRAB ROYAL

1/2 cup butter
1/3 cup finely chopped onion
1/3 cup finely chopped green pepper
3 7½-oz. cans Alaska King crab
1/2 cup mayonnaise
1 teaspoon Worcestershire sauce
2 teaspoons prepared mustard
1 teaspoon salt
1 Tablespoon parsley flakes

Saute onions and pepper in butter. Remove from heat and add crab, mayonnaise, parsley, Worcestershire, mustard and salt. Put in individual casserole dishes and sprinkle with paprika. Bake at 350° for 25 minutes.

FILLET OF SOLE

3 pounds fillet of sole
1 cup shrimp soup
1/4 cup parmesan cheese
salt and pepper

Put fillet of sole in 9X13 casserole. Pour soup over fish, and season with salt and pepper. Sprinkle parmesan cheese on top. Bake at 350° for 30 minutes. Serve directly from oven.

115

FRIED BASS

3 pounds bass fillets
1/2 cup prepared mustard
1½ cups yellow corn meal
salt and pepper

Salt and pepper fillets. Pour mustard over and mix with hands. Put cornmeal in bag, drop fillets in bag, and shake. Drop fillets in very hot deep fat for approximately 10 minutes or until done.

MIKE'S FISH FILLETS

fish fillets
salt
pepper
lemon and pepper seasoning salt
butter

Take clean fish fillets and place on plate, sides not touching. Season to taste with salt, pepper, and lemon and pepper seasoning. Put a pat of butter on top of each fillet and cook in microwave on high for 3 minutes. Turn and cook for another 3 minutes.

FRIED OYSTERS

1 egg
1 Tablespoon flour
4 Tablespoons milk
3 dozen oysters

Mix egg, flour, and milk. Beat until smooth and chill for 20 minutes. Dip oysters in batter and fry in deep, hot oil until golden brown.

SALMON CROQUETS

3 Tablespoons oil
1/3 cup flour
1 teaspoon salt
1/4 teaspoon celery salt
1/8 teaspoon pepper
1 cup milk plus 3 Tablespoons
1 16-oz. can salmon, drained
3 Tablespoons lemon juice
1 Tablespoon parsley
1 Tablespoon grated onion
1 egg, beaten
1 cup seasoned bread crumbs

Mix oil, flour, salt, celery salt, and pepper. Start to heat and gradually add 1 cup milk. Cook and stir over medium heat until thickened. Add flaked salmon to milk mixture, then add lemon juice, parsley and onion. Chill mixture and form into patties. Mix egg and 3 Tablespoons milk. Dip patties in egg mixture, roll in bread crumbs and fry for 4 minutes or until done.

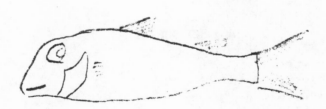

SALMON PATTIES

1 can salmon, drained
1 egg
1 small onion, chopped
cracker meal or bread crumbs

Mix together salmon, egg and onion. Form into patties and coat with meal or crumbs. Broil for 15 minutes or fry in shallow oil until brown.

117

SEAFOOD

SEAFOOD GUMBO

1/2 cup celery, chopped
1 large onion, chopped
1/4 cup bell pepper, chopped
1/8 teaspoon minced garlic
2 Tablespoons oil
1 small can tomato paste
2 Tablespoons cornstarch
2 4½-oz. cans shrimp
1 package frozen okra
1½ teaspoons salt
1/4 teaspoon thyme
dash hot sauce
1 small can crabmeat
1 small can clams
4 quarts chicken broth

Saute onion, peppers, celery, and garlic in oil. Add tomato paste and simmer for 10 minutes. Add okra, meat and spices and simmer for 10 more minutes. Add chicken broth and let simmer for 1½ hours. Use cornstarch mixed with a little water to thicken.

BOILED SHRIMP

2½ quarts water
2 cups celery, diced
1 cup onion, diced
2 lemons, sliced
1/8 teaspoon minced garlic
4 bay leaves
3 Tablespoons salt
1 Tablespoon whole allspice
1½ teaspoons cayenne pepper
3 pounds deheaded shrimp

In large stock pot, mix all ingredients except shrimp and bring to a boil. Reduce heat and simmer for 20 minutes. Add shrimp and cook until shrimp are pink and tender. Remove from heat and let set for 25 minutes. Remove shrimp from water, peel off shell, and remove veins. Serve over cracked ice with sauce.

118

SHRIMP CREOLE

1½ pounds small cleaned shrimp
2 Tablespoons butter
1/8 teaspoon minced garlic
2 large onions, diced
1 can tomatoes
1 can sliced mushrooms
2 cups celery, chopped
1 small jar pimento
1 Tablespoon chili powder
salt and pepper to taste
cornstarch to thicken
3 cups cooked rice

Saute garlic, onion, mushrooms, and celery in butter.
Add shrimp and cook 10 minutes. Add other ingredients
and cook until hot, adding rice last. Mix cornstarch
with a little water and slowly pour into mixture until
thickened to desired consistency.

SOUTHERN FRIED FISH

3 pounds fish, cut up
salt and pepper
1 cup yellow cornmeal

Heat deep fryer to very hot. Mix enough salt in
cornmeal until you can taste the salt, and pepper as
desired. Put cornmeal in paper sack, drop fish in a
few pieces at a time and shake to coat fish. Drop in
hot oil and fry until golden brown.

TUNA PATTIES

3 Tablespoons butter
2 Tablespoons flour
1/2 teaspoon salt
1/2 cup milk
1/4 cup grated onion
1 can tuna in spring water
2 cups cracker crumbs
3 eggs beaten

Mix butter with flour, salt, pepper, and milk. Cook over medium heat until thickened, stirring constantly. Cool. Add tuna and onion to sauce. Make patties, roll in cracker crumbs, dip in eggs, and roll in crumbs again. Chill through. Fry in hot cooking oil until brown.

TUNA-MACARONI SALAD

1 7-oz. package macaroni rings
2 or 3 6½-oz. cans tuna
2 eggs, hard-boiled and chopped
1 onion, chopped
1 small jar pimento, chopped
2 dill pickles, chopped
1/8 teaspoon dry mustard
1 Tablespoon dehydrated parsley flakes
1 10-oz. can green sweet peas
mayonnaise
paprika

Cook macaroni rings according to package directions. Drain and pour into large mixing bowl. Add all other ingredients through the green peas. Mix carefully. Use enough mayonnaise and pickle juice to mix well. Salt and pepper to taste. Garnish with boiled egg slices and paprika.

OTHER DESIRABLES

OTHER DESIRABLES

Wild Game

FRIED DOVE OR DUCK BREAST

dove or duck breasts
salt
pepper
flour

Salt and pepper meat. Coat with flour and place in hot oil. Brown fast on both sides. Reduce heat to medium and cook until tender. For variation: After browning, add sliced onions and water, cover and simmer for 1 hour.

DUCK GUMBO

2 ducks, boiled and deboned
3 bay leaves
1/4 teaspoon minced garlic
3/4 cup celery, chopped
2 large onions, chopped
1 bell pepper, chopped
1 package onion soup mix
2 Tablespoons oil
1 16-oz. can tomatoes
1/2 teaspoon black pepper
3 Tablespoons parsley flakes
1/2 teaspoon hot sauce
2 Tablespoons Worcestershire sauce
1 Tablespoon lemon juice
cornstarch

Mix all ingredients together, except cornstarch, and simmer for two hours. Use cornstarch to thicken if necessary. Pour over hot cooked white rice.

DUCK AND CUMIN RICE

1/2 cup onion, chopped
1/3 cup bell pepper, chopped
2 Tablespoons bacon drippings
1 cup uncooked rice
2 cans consomme
1 Tablespoon Worcestershire sauce
1/2 teaspoon salt
3/4 teaspoon cumin seed

Saute onions, pepper, and rice in bacon drippings until brown. Add consomme, Worcestershire, salt and cumin seed. Bring to a boil, stirring occasionally. Cover, reduce heat and simmer for 20 minutes.

DUCK

3 ducks
2 onions, quartered
2 carrots, chunked
1 stalk celery, chunked
2 apples, chunked
21 ounces consomme
1 cup dry sherry

Let ducks set overnight in salt water. Remove and dry. Rub outside of duck with salt and pepper and stuff cavities with part of vegetables and apples. Put ducks in roaster, add rest of vegetables and apples, consomme, 2 cans water and sherry. Bake at 350° for about 4 hours. Baste ducks often and turn twice while cooking. Strain juices after duck has cooked and thicken slightly with cornstarch mixed with a little water.

DUCK AND RICE

2 **wild ducks**
1 **can mushroom soup**
1 **cup raw rice**
1 **12—oz. can mixed vegetables**
1 **can chicken stock**
1 **cup celery, chopped**
1 **onion, quartered**

Boil ducks with onion. Save broth. When ducks are tender, debone and cut into small pieces. Cook rice in 2 cups water for 14 minutes. Cook vegetables and celery in chicken stock and 2 cups duck broth until tender. Add duck, vegetables and soup to rice. Simmer for 30 minutes on VERY LOW HEAT.

MARINATED DUCK BREASTS

4 **boneless duck breasts**
1/2 **cup Italian dressing**
1 **Tablespoon Worcestershire sauce**
juice of one lemon
1/4 **teaspoon garlic powder**
1/4 **teaspoon ground cloves**
bacon slices

Soak duck in salt water for 3 hours. Remove from water and drain on paper towel, pat dry and place in shallow pan. Combine all ingredients, pour over duck breasts and marinate for 4 hours. Wrap each breast in bacon and secure with toothpick. Cook on grill over a slow fire 7 minutes per side, or until bacon is done.

FROG LEGS

frog legs
salt
pepper
1 **egg**
1 **Tablespoon milk**
flour

Salt and pepper frog legs. Mix egg and milk. Dip frog legs in egg mixture, roll in flour and fry in hot oil until golden brown.

SOUTH DAKOTA PHEASANT

3 pheasants, cut up
1 can golden mushroom soup
2 cans cream of celery soup
1½ soup cans milk
salt and pepper to taste
flour

Coat pheasant in flour and brown in skillet until light brown. Mix soups and milk. Place pheasant in casserole and pour soup mixture over. Bake covered for 2 hours at 325°.

FRIED RABBIT

Cut rabbit into pieces. Boil slowly until tender. Salt and pepper rabbit to taste and roll in flour. Brown in hot oil.

SQUIRREL MULLIGAN

5 squirrels, boiled and deboned
6 potatoes
1 package frozen mixed vegetables
1 can chili without beans
1 bell pepper
1 pound ground beef
1 stick oleo
1 large can tomato paste
6 medium onions, chopped
4 Tablespoons sugar
1/2 teaspoon black pepper

Cook potatoes and mixed vegetables in separate pans, drain and mash. Mix all ingredients together, adding water enough to simmer for 2½ hours. Stir occasionally.

SQUIRREL—TEAL—OR WOOD DUCK

1 squirrel, teal or wood duck
2 medium potatoes, diced
2 onions, diced
3 stalks celery, diced
meat tenderizer
salt and pepper

Sprinkle meat liberally with tenderizer. Let set for 20 minutes. Place on heavy duty aluminum foil and pile vegetables on top. Salt and pepper to taste. Seal foil tightly and bake for 1½ hours at 325°.

BRAISED VENISON

2 cups flour
2 teaspoons salt
1 teaspoon pepper
1 onion, cut in rings
garlic salt
2 Tablespoons fat
2 cups water
8 venison steaks

Soak venison overnight in 1 quart water and 1/4 cup salt. Mix together flour, salt and pepper. Coat steaks with flour mixture and brown. Lay onion rings on top of browned steaks and sprinkle with garlic salt. Add water and simmer for 1 hour.

POP BILL'S VENISON STEAK

venison steak, 1/2 inch thick maximum
meat tenderizer
margarine
pepper (optional)

Soak in cold water overnight. Change water twice, squeezing water from meat each time. When ready to cook, squeeze water from meat, blot dry on paper towel, and apply meat tenderizer. Let set 20 minutes. Heat iron skillet to 400°. Put 1/4 stick margarine in skillet and immediately add steak. Cook for 45 seconds on each side.

POLYNESIAN VENISON

1 pound venison steaks
1/4 cup flour
1/4 cup margarine
1/2 cup boiling water
1 teaspoon salt
3 bell peppers
3/4 cup chunked pineapple

Cut steaks in cubes. Flour and brown in oil. Add water and salt and simmer until meat is tender. Cut peppers in strips and add to meat along with pineapple chunks. Cover with the following sauce.

SAUCE

3 Tablespoons cornstarch
3/4 cup pineapple juice
1/4 cup vinegar
1/2 cup sugar
1 Tablespoon soy sauce

Mix all ingredients and cook until thickened over medium heat, stirring constantly. Pour over meat mixture and simmer for 20 minutes. Serve over white or fried rice.

OTHER DESIRABLES

Vegetables

and

Casseroles

BOILED ARTICHOKES

2 artichokes
1 Tablespoon olive oil
2 Tablespoons lemon juice
2 Tablespoons salt

Trim artichoke stems and place in pan of water that covers artichokes completely and add all seasonings. Boil until a center leaf pulls out easily. Drain water, set in small bowl and serve with melted butter.

ASPARAGUS CASSEROLE

1 large can asparagus
3 eggs, hard-boiled
1/4 teaspoon salt
1/2 cup milk
1 can cream of mushroom soup
1/2 cup grated cheese
1 Tablespoon butter

Put asparagus in bottom of buttered casserole. Add chopped eggs. Combine milk, salt and soup, mix well and pour over asparagus. Sprinkle top with cheese and bake at 350° for 20 to 25 minutes.

RICE AND ASPARAGUS CASSEROLE

3/4 cup uncooked rice
1 15-oz. can asparagus
1 can cream of mushroom soup
grated cheese

Cook rice. Add asparagus with juice and soup. Stir well and place in baking dish and cover with grated cheese. Bake at 350° until heated thoroughly and cheese is melted.

ASPARAGUS AND SOUR CREAM

2 pounds fresh asparagus
1 8-oz. carton sour cream
1 egg yolk, hard-boiled

Boil asparagus until tender. Arrange on platter, pour sour cream over evenly and garnish with finely grated egg yolk.

AU GRATIN POTATOES

3 Tablespoons butter
2 Tablespoons flour
1 teaspoon salt
1 cup milk
1 cup cheddar cheese, grated
3 cups potatoes, thinly sliced

Potatoes should be boiled until tender crisp. Mix butter, flour, salt and milk and cook until thickened stirring constantly. Add cheese and let melt. Place potatoes in buttered casserole dish and cover with sauce. Bake at 350° for 40 minutes.

BAKED BEANS WITH HAMBURGER

1 pound ground beef
3/4 cup chopped onion
1/2 cup chopped bell pepper
1/2 cup catsup
1/2 teaspoon salt
dash hot sauce
1/4 teaspoon pepper
2 cans pork and beans (1 pound)
1 Tablespoon prepared mustard
3 Tablespoons brown sugar
1 Tablespoon Worcestershire sauce
1 can tomatoes with green chilies

Brown meat with onion and bell pepper. Mix with all other ingredients and bake in buttered casserole for 30 minutes at 375°.

BAKED NAVY BEANS

2 cups navy or great northern beans
1 Tablespoon soda
3 Tablespoons salt
5 Tablespoons brown sugar
1 Tablespoon prepared mustard
1 onion, chopped
1 bell pepper, chopped

Soak beans in soda water overnight. Drain and recover with water. Simmer until just before beans are tender. Drain all but 1 cup water and mix in other ingredients. Cover and bake at 350° for 1 hour or until beans are tender.

COUNTRY BEETS

Wash beets. Cut tops to 1-inch long and leave on roots. Place in 325° oven until tender. When tender, cut tops and roots off and peel. Serve with melted butter.

HARVARD BEETS

1/2 cup vinegar
1/2 Tablespoon cornstarch
1/2 cup sugar
2 cups beets, cooked and sliced
2 Tablespoons butter

Cook vinegar, sugar, and cornstarch for five minutes over medium heat. Add beets and cook for 30 minutes on very low heat. Just before taking off stove, turn heat on high and let beets come to a boil. Add butter and serve.

ALMOND BROCCOLI

2 packages frozen broccoli, cooked
1/2 cup mayonnaise
1 Tablespoon lemon juice
3/4 cup American cheese, grated
1 can cream of mushroom soup
1 cup crushed round snack crackers
1/4 cup slivered almonds

Place broccoli in casserole dish. Mix all ingredients except cheese, cracker crumbs, and almonds and pour over broccoli. Top with cheese, cracker crumbs and almonds. Bake at 350° until hot and cheese melts.

BROCCOLI CASSEROLE

3 cups hot cooked rice
1 package chopped frozen broccoli, cooked
1 can cream of chicken soup
3 Tablespoons oleo
1 cup each onions and celery, chopped
1 teaspoon salt
1 8-oz. jar processed cheese spread

Run hot water from tap over jar of cheese to soften. Saute onions and celery in butter. Mix everything together, put in buttered casserole and bake at 350° for 30 minutes.

BUTTERED CARROTS

1 quart sliced carrots
1/3 cup butter
1/2 teaspoon salt
1 teaspoon sugar
1/8 teaspoon pepper

Boil carrots just until they start to get tender. Drain water, add other ingredients, cover and cook 10 more minutes over low heat.

BRUSSELS SPROUTS AU GRATIN

2 packages frozen brussels sprouts
1/2 cup milk
1 Tablespoon butter
1 Tablespoon flour
3/4 cup grated cheddar cheese
1/2 cup round snack cracker crumbs
1 teaspoon parsley flakes

Combine milk, butter, flour and parsley in saucepan and heat until thickened. Cook brussels sprouts by package directions and put in casserole dish. Cover with white sauce, season with salt and pepper, sprinkle with cheese and cracker crumbs. Bake at 350° for 30 minutes.

CAULIFLOWER CASSEROLE

1 head cauliflower, washed and separated
1½ teaspoons salt
1/8 teaspoon minced garlic
1 can tomatoes
1 teaspoon dry parsley flakes
1/4 cup grated cheddar cheese

Cook cauliflower in salted water until tender. Add other ingredients in order except cheese. Place in buttered casserole, layer cheese on top and bake for 15 minutes at 350° or until cheese melts.

CREAMED CAULIFLOWER

1 head cauliflower, broken up
1/2 cup evaporated milk
1 teaspoon salt
2 Tablespoons butter

Cook cauliflower until tender crisp. Remove from heat and drain water to 1/2 cup. Add milk, butter and salt. Return to stove and heat for 5 minutes.

MICROWAVE CORN ON COB

Leave corn in shuck. Cut both ends off and place in microwave for approximately 3 minutes per ear or until corn is tender.

EGGPLANT CASSEROLE

1 eggplant, peeled and sliced
1 onion, finely chopped
1/2 teaspoon salt
1/4 teaspoon pepper
1 egg, beaten
1/2 cup milk
3/4 cup mild cheddar cheese, grated
3/4 cup crumbled cornbread
2 chopped tomatoes

Boil eggplant till tender. Mash and add to onion and seasonings. Beat together egg and milk. Combine all ingredients together with tomatoes, cheese and cornbread. Bake in buttered casserole dish at 350° for 30 to 40 minutes.

HASH BROWN POTATO CASSEROLE

1 32-oz. bag frozen, shredded hash browns, thawed
½ cup butter, melted
½ cup onion, chopped
1 can cream of chicken soup
1 8-oz. carton sour cream
1 cup grated cheddar cheese
2 cups corn flakes, crushed

Combine potatoes, ¼ cup butter, onion, soup, sour cream and cheese. Stir well and spoon into a 2½ quart buttered casserole dish. Mix remaining butter with corn flakes and sprinkle over potatoes. Bake at 350° for 50 minutes.

FRIED OKRA

5 cups sliced okra
1½ teaspoons salt
1/2 teaspoon pepper
1/2 cup flour
1/2 cup cornmeal

Put dry ingredients in plastic bag and shake to mix. Add okra all at one time and shake to coat. Pour in skillet with 1 inch hot oil and fry fast until brown and crisp.

ONION FRIES

3/4 cup self-rising flour
1/2 teaspoon baking powder
1 Tablespoon cornmeal
1/2 cup non-fat dry milk
2 teaspoons sugar
1/2 teaspoon salt
2½ cups chopped onion

Combine all ingredients except onions. Add cold water a little at a time until you have a very thick batter. Add onions and mix well. Make small half dollar size patties by dropping from spoon into hot shallow oil and flattening slightly with back of spoon. Brown on both sides.

BAKED ONIONS AND PEPPERS

1/2 onion per serving
1/2 bell pepper per serving
1 teaspoon butter per two servings
salt and pepper

Quarter onions and peppers. Place in aluminum foil, salt and pepper and place pats of butter on top. Seal aluminum foil tightly. Bake at 400° for 30 to 45 minutes or until onions and peppers are tender. Great with steak.

GLAZED CARROTS

2 cups sliced carrots
3/4 cups water
1/2 teaspoon salt
2 Tablespoons butter
1 teaspoon sugar
7 large marshmallows

Combine all ingredients in a saucepan. Cook slowly until carrots are tender and are in a light to medium syrup.

GREEN BEAN CASSEROLE

2 cans French cut green beans
2 slices bacon, fried and crumbled
1 can cream of mushroom soup
1 Tablespoon caraway seeds
1½ teaspoons salt
1 cup grated cheese
1/2 cup round snack cracker crumbs

Cook beans slowly in their own juice for 15 minutes with crumbled bacon and bacon drippings. Pour off liquid, add caraway seed, mushroom soup and salt. Place in 9X13 baking dish layering green beans and grated cheese for two layers each, putting cracker crumbs on top. Dot with butter and bake for 30 minutes at 325°.

FRIED GREEN BEANS

1 can green beans
3 slices bacon
1 medium onion, chopped
2 Tablespoons vinegar
1 teaspoon salt
dash pepper

Cut bacon in small pieces and fry along with onion. Let onion get clear, then add all other ingredients. Cover and cook slowly for 45 minutes.

GREEN BEAN AU GRATIN

4 Tablespoons butter
4 Tablespoons flour
1 teaspoon salt
1/4 teaspoon dry mustard
1½ cups milk
3/4 cup cheddar cheese, grated
2 cans French style green beans
1/3 cup parmesan cheese
slivered almonds

In saucepan, melt butter and add flour, salt and mustard. Bring to a slow boil and turn heat to simmer. Add milk and cook until mixture thickens, stirring constantly. Add cheese until melted. Put drained beans in bottom of buttered casserole. Pour sauce over and stir slightly. Sprinkle with parmesan cheese and almonds. Bake at 350° for 30 minutes.

MEXICAN HOMINY

1/2 stick oleo
1 onion, diced
2 cans white hominy
2 jalapeno peppers, finely chopped
1/2 teaspoon salt
1/2 teaspoon pepper
1 cup processed cheese, grated

Saute onions in butter. Add remaining ingredients using 3/4 cup cheese. Put in casserole dish, sprinkling remaining cheese on top. Bake at 350° for 20 to 30 minutes or until hot and cheese is melted.

SAUTED MUSHROOMS

1 pound small mushrooms
4 Tablespoons butter
2 Tablespoons Worcestershire sauce

Put all ingredients in a skillet and cook over medium heat until tender and start to turn brown.

PEAS CONTINENTAL

1 cup sliced, fresh or canned mushrooms
1/4 cup onions, minced
2 Tablespoons margarine
1/4 teaspoon salt
dash pepper
1/4 teaspoon nutmeg
1/8 teaspoon dried marjoram
2 Tablespoons sherry
2 cups English peas, cooked and drained

Saute mushrooms and onion in margarine until tender.
Add next five ingredients, then hot peas.

MEXICAN CABBAGE

1 large onion, diced
2 Tablespoons butter
1 can tomatoes
1 head cabbage, cut up to boil
1 jalapeno pepper, finely chopped
salt and pepper

Saute onion in butter. Add other ingredients and cook
over slow heat until cabbage is tender.

SCALLOPED POTATOES

6 large potatoes
4 Tablespoons butter
3 Tablespoons flour
3 cups milk
1½ teaspoons salt
1/4 teaspoon pepper
1/4 cup onions, chopped
1/2 cup cheddar cheese, grated

Peel and slice potatoes thin. Mix butter, salt,
pepper, flour, milk and cheese. Put half of potato
slices into greased casserole. Pour in half the sauce
and onions. Put in other half of potatoes, then sauce
and onions. Cover and bake at 350° for 1 hour.
Uncover and let brown slightly.

COUNTRY FRIED POTATOES

4 medium raw potatoes, peeled
1 medium onion, chopped
1¼ teaspoons salt
1/4 teaspoon pepper

Heat about 1/4-inch oil in skillet. Cut potatoes in french fry like strips and put in hot oil with onion. Salt and pepper. Stir potatoes occasionally but let brown and cook until tender.

POTATOES IN CREAM

4 cups diced cooked potatoes
1/2 teaspoon salt
1/4 cup butter
1/8 teaspoon pepper
minced parsley
2 cups light cream

Combine ingredients except parsley in large skillet. Cook slowly until cream is slightly thickened and potatoes hot. Sprinkle with parsley.

QUICK SCALLOPED POTATOES

4 cups diced raw potatoes
1 cup minced onion
2 teaspoons salt
1/2 cup boiling water
1/2 cup milk
1/2 cup grated cheese
2 Tablespoons chopped parsley

Combine first four ingredients together in saucepan and cook covered for 10 minutes. Uncover and simmer, stirring occasionally, until water is almost evaporated. Add milk, cheese and a dash of pepper. Heat until cheese melts and add parsley.

CANDIED SWEET POTATOES

3 pounds sweet potatoes
1/4 cup butter
3/4 cup light brown sugar, packed
3/4 cup white sugar
1 teaspoon salt
1/2 cup water

Cut potatoes in large chunks. Arrange in buttered casserole. Sift, then blend sugars and salt together and sprinkle over potatoes. Pour water over and cook at 325° for 20 minutes, turn potatoes and cook another 20 minutes. Potatoes should be tender and in heavy syrup.

COUNTRY BAKED SWEET POTATOES

Wash small to medium sweet potatoes. Rub skins with butter and place in 375° oven until tender. Serve as you would white baked potato with butter, salt and pepper.

SWEET POTATO CASSEROLE

3 cups sweet potatoes
1/2 cup milk
1/2 teaspoon vanilla
1/2 cup butter
2 eggs
1 cup sugar
1 cup brown sugar
1/3 cup butter
1/3 cup flour
1/2 cup chopped nuts
1 package miniature marshmallows

Cook and mash sweet potatoes and add next five ingredients. Mix next four ingredients together for topping. Layer potato mixture, miniature marshmallows, potato mixture, miniature marshmallows and topping mix. Bake at 350° for 35 minutes.

143

GLAZED SWEET POTATOES

4 medium sweet potatoes, cooked and hot
1/4 cup melted butter
1/2 cup brown sugar

Slice peeled potatoes in halves lengthwise. Arrange in baking dish and spread a mixture of the butter and brown sugar combined. Broil until delicately browned and glazed – about 8 minutes.

BARBECUED RICE

3 cups cooked rice
1 medium onion, chopped
1/2 cup celery, chopped
1 can cream of chicken soup
1 can cream of mushroom soup
1 can chicken broth
1½ teaspoons liquid smoke
1/2 teaspoon salt
1/8 teaspoon pepper

Mix all ingredients together and put in buttered casserole. Bake for 30 to 40 minutes at 350°.

COOKED WHITE RICE

2½ cups water
1 cup rice
1 teaspoon butter
1 teaspoon salt

Add salt and butter to water and bring to a boil. Add rice and stir. Turn fire down until rice is cooking at a slow boil and stir again. Cook uncovered until water has cooked out and rice is almost dry. Cover, remove from heat and let steam for 30 minutes. Do not lift lid while rice is steaming. After 30 minutes put rice in collander and rinse with hot water.

BROWN RICE

1 cup brown rice
1 teaspoon salt
2½ cups water
1 Tablespoon butter

Put all ingredients in saucepan and cover. Bring to a fast boil stirring twice. Reduce heat and simmer covered for 45 to 50 minutes. Take off heat and leave covered for another 20 minutes.

BROWN RICE ROYAL

2 cups sliced mushrooms
1/2 cup finely chopped green onions
2 Tablespoons butter
1 teaspoon salt
3 cups cooked rice, cooked in beef broth

Saute mushrooms and onions in butter until onions are clear. Add rice and salt and heat thoroughly.

FRIED RICE

1 cup uncooked rice
2½ cups water
2 bouillon cubes, beef or chicken
1 Tablespoon butter
2 eggs
1/3 cup soy sauce
1/2 cup chopped meat
1 small onion, finely chopped

Bring to a boil: water, butter and bouillon cubes. Add rice and cook at high temperature until water has cooked out, but before rice sticks. Cover, remove from heat and let steam for 30 minutes. Scramble eggs slowly with onion and meat in large skillet. Add steamed rice and mix together frying in skillet. Fry until rice starts to brown, add soy sauce and fry stirring for several minutes. More soy sauce can be used if desired. Meat can be chicken, bacon, ham or pork chop.

145

RICE CONSOMME

1 cup raw rice
1 can beef consomme
1 can water
1/4 cup butter
1/2 package onion soup mix
1 small can sliced mushrooms

Combine all ingredients together in casserole dish. Cover and bake in preheated oven at 350° for 1 hour, stirring every 15 minutes. Be sure oven is preheated.

SPANISH RICE

6 slices bacon
1/2 cup bell pepper, diced
1 cup onion, diced
1 jalapeno pepper, finely chopped
1 can tomatoes
1 cup rice
3/4 cup water
3/4 teaspoon salt
1 teaspoon sugar
2 teaspoons chili powder

Cook bacon until crisp. Saute onion and pepper in bacon drippings and add remaining ingredients. Crumble bacon and mix well. Bring to a boil, reduce heat, cover and cook until rice is done. Stir often.

SOUTHERN FRIED SQUASH

4 medium yellow squash, sliced
1/2 cup oil
1 large onion, chopped
salt and pepper

Heat skillet with shallow oil. Put squash and onions into skillet. Salt and pepper to taste. Cover and fry over medium to high heat until turning brown and tender. May sift 1/4 cup flour before starting to cook to help brown.

146

FRIED SQUASH, GREEN TOMATOES, OR EGG PLANT

Slice vegetables in thin slices. Salt, pepper and flour. Fry individually in shallow hot grease until brown on one side, turn and brown other side.

YELLOW SQUASH CASSEROLE

2 cups cooked yellow squash
3/4 stick oleo
1/2 teaspoon pepper
1 cup American cheese, grated
1 small can evaporated milk
2 cups cracker crumbs
2 eggs, beaten
1 teaspoon salt
1 cup onion, chopped

Mix all ingredients together. Put in buttered casserole dish. Add more cheese on top if desired. Bake for 40 minutes at 350°.

ZUCCHINI OR YELLOW SQUASH CASSEROLE

3 medium diced squash
3/4 cup celery, diced
3/4 cup onion, diced
1/2 cup butter
1½ cups water
1 teaspoon salt
1/2 teaspoon pepper
2 eggs, beaten
2 cups seasoned bread crumbs
1 cup cheddar cheese, grated

Boil all vegetables in water and butter for 5 minutes. Add other ingredients and mix well until cheese melts. Put in baking dish and bake for 30 minutes at 350°.

147

VEGETABLES AND CASSEROLES

STIR-FRY VEGETABLES

1 large zucchini
1 large onion, chopped
1 Tablespoon oleo
1/2 cup soy sauce
1/4 teaspoon salt

Cut zucchini in strips about 1/4-inch thick and 3 inches long. Put in skillet with onion and oleo. Stir fry until onion starts to get clear. Add soy sauce and salt. Cook until zucchini and onions are tender crisp.

STEWED OKRA AND TOMATOES

1 onion, chopped
2 Tablespoons oil
1 package frozen okra
1 can tomatoes
1/4 teaspoon pepper
1/2 teaspoon salt

Cook onion in oil till browned. Add remaining ingredients and cook until okra in tender and mixture thickens. (10 to 15 minutes) Stir occasionally.

BROILED TOMATOES

3 tomatoes
salt
pepper
sugar
butter
parmesan cheese
seasoned bread crumbs

Core tomatoes, cut in half crosswise and put sliced side up in casserole dish. Sprinkle with salt, pepper and sugar. Place 5 inches from broiler and broil for approximately 10 minutes. Mix just enough butter with bread crumbs to hold together. Put on top of tomatoes and generously sprinkle with parmesan cheese. Broil 3 to 4 more minutes.

VEGETABLE CASSEROLE

1 small can English peas
1 small can lima beans
1 large can French style green beans
2 cups mayonnaise
4 eggs, hard-boiled and chopped
1 medium onion, diced
1 Tablespoon dry mustard
1 Tablespoon Worcestershire sauce
6 Tablespoons oil
dash hot sauce
1/4 teaspoon garlic salt
1 Tablespoon lemon juice

Drain all vegetables. Combine remaining ingredients adding eggs last. Layer in deep casserole dish as follows: Peas, sauce, lima beans, sauce, green beans and sauce. Bake at 400° until hot through.

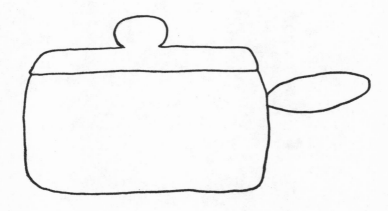

OTHER DESIRABLES

Cakes
and
Icings

APPLE CAKE

2 cups sifted flour
2 cups sugar
1¼ cups cooking oil
2 eggs
1 teaspoon salt
1 teaspoon soda
1 teaspoon cinnamon
2 teaspoons vanilla
1 cup chopped nuts
3 cups apples, peeled and chopped

Combine flour, sugar, oil and eggs. Beat until smooth. Add apples, salt, soda, cinnamon and vanilla. Mix well and stir in nuts. Bake at 325° for 45 minutes in greased 9X13 pan.

MOM'S RAW APPLE CAKE

2 cups flour
2 teaspoons soda
1 teaspoon baking powder
1 teaspoon salt
2 cups sugar
3 Tablespoons milk
2 eggs
1 cup oil
2 teaspoons vanilla
1 cup pecans, chopped
4 large apples, diced

Combine all ingredients in large mixing bowl. Bake in 9X13 pan for 45-50 minutes at 350°. This cake will be very moist and gooey.

BANANA SPLIT CAKE

CRUST: 1 cup powdered sugar
2 cups graham cracker crumbs
1 stick butter, melted

CUSTARD: 1 cup powdered sugar
2 eggs
2 sticks butter

TOPPING: 2 bananas, sliced
2 Tablespoons lemon juice
1 large can crushed pineapple, drained
1/2 cup chopped pecans
1 carton frozen whipped topping

Mix ingredients for crust and press in bottom of square pan. Mix custard ingredients and beat well for 15 minutes. Pour into crust. Stir sliced bananas in lemon juice to keep from turning dark. Layer on top of custard along with pineapple. Top with whipped topping and nuts. This must be kept refrigerated.

BROWNIES

3/4 cup flour
3/4 cup sugar
1/4 cup cocoa
1/2 teaspoon baking powder
1/4 teaspoon salt
1/4 cup milk
2/3 stick butter, melted
1 egg
1 teaspoon vanilla
1/2 cup chopped nuts

Mix everything together in order given. Bake at 350° for 25 minutes. Make sure oven is preheated.

CRUSHED BANANA CAKE

1/2 cup butter
2 eggs
1½ cups sugar
1/2 cup sour milk
2 teaspoons baking powder
2 cups flour
3 bananas, mashed
1 teaspoon soda

Mix all ingredients together well. Bake at 350° in two layer cake pans until done. Ice with cream cheese icing.

CREAM CHEESE ICING

1 Tablespoon butter
1 8-oz. package cream cheese
1/2 box powdered sugar
3 Tablespoons strong black coffee
1/2 cup chopped pecans

Stir together and ice cooled cake.

BLONDE BROWNIES

2 cups all-purpose flour
1/4 teaspoon soda
1 teaspoon baking powder
1 teaspoon salt
2 cups firmly packed brown sugar
2/3 cup shortening, melted
2 eggs, slightly beaten
2 teaspoons vanilla
1 cup chocolate chips
1/3 cup nuts, chopped

Mix flour, soda, baking powder and salt. Add sugar to shortening and mix well. Blend in eggs and vanilla. Add flour mixture gradually, mixing well. Spread in 9X13 pan. Sprinkle with chips and nuts. Bake at 350° for 30 minutes. Cool in pan and cut in bars.

BROWNIE PUDDING

3/4 cup flour
1½ teaspoons baking powder
1 rounded Tablespoon cocoa
2 Tablespoons oil
1/2 teaspoon salt
1/2 cup sugar
1/3 cup milk
1 teaspoon vanilla
1/2 cup nuts, chopped (optional)

Mix all together and put in greased 9X9 square baker.

Mix together 1/2 cup brown sugar, 1/2 cup white sugar, 3 Tablespoons cocoa, and sprinkle over mixture in baker. Pour 2 cups boiling water over all. Bake at 350° for 30-40 minutes. Good with ice cream.

EASY QUICK BROWNIES

2 6-oz. packages semi-sweet chocolate chips
1 can sweetened condensed milk
2 Tablespoons flour
dash salt
2 teaspoons vanilla
2 cups chopped nuts

Mix all ingredients together and spread in well-greased 9X9 pan. Bake at 350° for 30 minutes.

GOOD CHOCOLATE BROWNIES

3/4 cup sifted flour
1 cup sugar
5 Tablespoons cocoa
1/2 teaspoon salt
1/2 cup oil
2 eggs
1 teaspoon vanilla
3/4 cup pecans, chopped

Mix thoroughly all ingredients, making certain sugar is dissolved. Bake in 9X9 square pan for 25 to 30 minutes in preheated 350° oven.

PAT'S BROWNIES

1/2 cup flour
2 eggs
1 teaspoon vanilla
1/2 teaspoon salt
1 cup sugar
2 squares semi-sweet chocolate
1 stick margarine

Mix dry ingredients. Melt butter and chocolate and mix with dry ingredients. Pour into greased 9X9-inch pan and bake at 350° for 30 minutes.

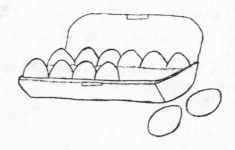

PEANUT BUTTER BROWNIES

1 cup crunchy peanut butter
1/2 cup butter
2 cups firmly packed light brown sugar
1 cup sifted flour
3 eggs
1 teaspoon vanilla
1/2 teaspoon salt

Beat peanut butter and butter in large mixing bowl until well blended. Add sugar, eggs and vanilla. Beat until light and fluffy. Stir in flour and salt. Spread batter into 9X13 greased pan and bake at 350° for 30 to 35 minutes.

L'S BUTTERMILK CAKE

2 cups sugar
3/4 cup shortening
3 eggs
2 cups flour
1 teaspoon baking powder
1/2 teaspoon soda
1/8 teaspoon salt
1 cup buttermilk
1 teaspoon almond flavoring
1 teaspoon vanilla

Cream sugar and shortening. Beat in eggs, one at a time. Sift dry ingredients and blend with sugar and shortening, alternately with buttermilk and flavorings. Bake in tube pan for 1 hour at 350°.

CARROT CAKE

4 eggs, well beaten
2 cups sugar
1½ cups oil
1 cup chopped nuts
2 cups grated carrots
3 cups flour
3 teaspoons baking powder
2 teaspoons soda
2 teaspoons cinnamon

Sift dry ingredients together four times. Mix all other ingredients in separate bowl, then slowly blend together. Bake in large square pan or two round layer pans that have been greased and floured, at 350° for 1 hour.

CAKES

CHOCOLATE CHIP SQUARES

1 stick butter
1/2 cup sugar
1/2 cup brown sugar
1 egg
1/2 teaspoon vanilla
1¼ cups flour
1/2 teaspoon salt
1/2 teaspoon soda
1/2 cup chopped pecans
1 6-oz. package chocolate chips

Cream together butter and sugars. Add remaining
ingredients in order given. Bake in 9X13 inch pan at
350° for 20 to 25 minutes.

CHEESE CAKE

1 stick oleo, softened
1 cup flour
1/4 cup light brown sugar
1/2 cup pecans, chopped
1 8-oz. package cream cheese
1/3 cup lemon juice
1 can sweetened condensed milk

Combine first four ingredients and press in large pie
pan and bake at 400° until light brown. Beat together
cheese, juice, and milk until thick. Pour into above
crust. Chill until set and top with any pie filling.

CHOCOLATE SHEET CAKE

2 cups sugar
2 cups flour
1 stick oleo
4 Tablespoons cocoa
1 cup water
1/2 cup oil
1/2 cup buttermilk
1 teaspoon soda
2 eggs
1 teaspoon vanilla

Mix sugar and flour and set aside. Combine next four ingredients and bring to a boil. Pour over sugar and flour and stir. Add remaining ingredients and mix well. Spray sheet cake pan with vegetable spray, pour in batter and bake at 400° for 20-25 minutes.

FROSTING

1 stick oleo
4 Tablespoons cocoa
6 Tablespoons milk
1 box powdered sugar
1 cup nuts, chopped
1 teaspoon vanilla

Mix butter, cocoa, and milk in saucepan and bring to a boil. Take off stove and add last three ingredients and beat until smooth. Spread over cake as soon as it comes from oven.

EGGLESS-MILKLESS CHOCOLATE CAKE

1½ cups flour
1 cup sugar
3 Tablespoons cocoa
1 teaspoon soda
1/2 teaspoon salt
1 teaspoon vanilla
1 teaspoon vinegar
6 Tablespoons oil
1 cup water

Mix all ingredients together and bake in 9X13-inch pan at 350° for 25-30 minutes.

ICING

1 cup sugar
1/3 cup milk
1/2 stick oleo
2½ teaspoons cocoa
1 teaspoon vanilla

Cook 2 minutes after this boils. Test for soft ball in cold water. Remove from heat and beat until stiff enough to spread on cake.

COCONUT CAKE

2 cups sugar
1 cup shortening
5 eggs
2 cups self-rising flour
1 cup buttermilk
1 small can flaked coconut
1½ teaspoons coconut flavoring

Cream together sugar, shortening and eggs. Add remaining ingredients, mixing thoroughly. Bake in ungreased 9X13 pan for 1 hour at 350°

COCONUT CAKE

1 white or yellow cake mix
3 eggs
1 cup oil
1 8½-oz. can cream of coconut
1 small carton sour cream
1 teaspoon vanilla

Mix all ingredients in order given.   Pour into well-greased and floured bundt pan.   Bake for 45 minutes at 350°.

THE DEMON'S FLOAT

1 cup flour
1/4 teaspoon salt
3/4 cup sugar
2 teaspoons baking powder
1¼ Tablespoons cocoa
1/2 cup milk
2 Tablespoons oleo, melted
1 teaspoon vanilla
1/2 cup chopped nuts

SAUCE

1/2 cup granulated sugar
1/2 cup brown sugar
4½ Tablespoons cocoa
1 cup boiling water

Sift cake flour, salt, sugar, baking powder, and cocoa together.   Add milk, butter, vanilla and nuts. Mix well and pour into well greased 9X9 baking dish and cover with hot sauce mixture. Bake at 350° for 40 minutes. Serve with whipped cream.

161

FLORA'S NAMELESS CAKE

1 Devils food cake mix
1 can cherry pie filling
3 eggs

Stir together by hand. Pour into greased and floured 9X13 pan and bake for 30 minutes at 350°.

GLAZE

1 cup evaporated milk
1 cup granulated sugar
5 Tablespoons butter
1 6-oz. package chocolate chips

Bring to a boil and cook for 1 minute stirring constantly. Make holes in cake with fork and glaze while both are hot.

FUNNEL CAKES

2 eggs
1-1/3 cups milk
2-2/3 cups flour
4 Tablespoons sugar
1/2 teaspoon salt
1 teaspoon baking powder
2 teaspoons baking soda

Beat eggs and milk together. Sift dry ingredients twice and add to milk mixture. Beat until smooth. Cover the hole in a funnel with index finger and fill with batter. Hold funnel over preheated oil and move funnel in a circle or figure eight, filling to center of circles. Cover hole in funnel when you want to stop cake. Fry, turning once to get golden brown on both sides. Sift lightly with powdered sugar while hot.

FRUIT COCKTAIL CAKE

1½ cups sugar
2 cups flour
1 teaspoon vanilla
2 eggs
1/2 teaspoon soda
1/2 teaspoon baking powder
1 can fruit cocktail
1/2 cup coconut
1/2 cup chopped nuts

Mix well in order given, pour into 9X13 pan and bake for 30-35 minutes at 350°.

FRUIT COCKTAIL CAKE ICING

1½ cups sugar
1 stick butter
1 small can evaporated milk
1 teaspoon vanilla
1/2 cup coconut
1/2 cup chopped nuts

Combine first four ingredients and cook until well mixed. Add coconut and nuts. Ice cake while hot.

HAZEL CAKE

1 box yellow butter cake mix
4 eggs
3/4 cup oil
1/2 cup sugar
1 small box sour cream
1 Tablespoon cinnamon
4 Tablespoons brown sugar
1 cup chopped nuts

Mix first five ingredients together. Pour half of mixture into bottom of well greased and floured bundt pan. Mix cinnamon, brown sugar, and nuts. Sprinkle this over batter in pan and cover with remaining batter. Bake for 45-50 minutes at 350°.

163

CAKES

L & D CAKE

LIGHT PART:
- 1 cup sugar
- 1/2 cup butter, soft
- 1½ cups flour
- 1/2 cup milk
- 4 egg whites
- 1 teaspoon baking powder
- 1 teaspoon vanilla

Mix together and bake in two greased and floured layer cake pans at 325° for 40-45 minutes. These will be thin layers.

DARK PART:
- 1 cup sugar
- 1/2 cup butter, soft
- 1/2 cup milk
- 2 cups flour
- 1/2 cup red syrup
- 4 egg yolks
- 1 teaspoon cinnamon
- 1/2 teaspoon nutmeg
- 1 teaspoon allspice
- 1 teaspoon baking powder
- 1 cup chopped pecans

Mix together and bake in 2 greased and floured layer cake pans at 325° for 40-45 minutes. These will be thick layers.

FILLING:
- 3 cups sugar
- 1½ cups milk
- 1/4 cup butter
- 1 package coconut
- 1 cup chopped pecans
- 1 package chopped dates

Combine first three ingredients and cook for 11 minutes. Add last three ingredients and take off stove. Start with dark layer, add filling, light layer, filling, etc.

164

LEMON CAKE

1 box white or yellow cake mix
1 package lemon instant pudding mix
1/2 cup oil
1 cup milk
4 eggs
1 teaspoon vanilla

Mix together thoroughly. Bake in oblong cake pan or 2 layer pans that have been greased and floured. Bake at 350° for 35 minutes.

LEMON PUDDING CAKE

1 white or yellow cake mix, prepared and baked
1 package lemon flavored gelatin
2 cups boiling water
1 package instant lemon pudding mix, prepared
1 package whipped topping, whipped

While cake bakes, dissolve gelatin in boiling water. When cake is done, remove from oven and punch holes with fork all through cake, about one inch apart. Spoon hot gelatin solution evenly over hot cake. Place in refrigerator until chilled. Prepare pudding mix, according to package directions, let partially set (3-5 minutes) and spread over chilled cake. Return cake to refrigerator until pudding is firmly set. Whip topping mix with milk and vanilla according to package directions, and spread over pudding layer. Store covered in refrigerator. Best if sets overnight. Cake should be baked in 9X13 pan.

LEMON BUNDT CAKE

1 lemon cake mix
1 box instant lemon pudding
1 cup plus 2 Tablespoons water
4 eggs
1/2 cup oil
1 cup powdered sugar
1 lemon

Combine all ingredients except sugar and lemon in bowl. Beat at low speed for 3 minutes. Grease and flour bundt pan. Bake at 350° for 40 minutes. Glaze with 1 cup powdered sugar and juice of 1 lemon.

MANDARIN ORANGE CAKE

1 yellow butter cake mix
3/4 cup oil
4 eggs
1 can mandarin oranges, drained

Mix and bake in two round greased and floured can pans at 350° for 30-35 minutes.

ICING

1 20-oz. can crushed pineapple, not drained
1 small box vanilla instant pudding mix
1 9-oz. carton frozen whipped topping

Fold together gently and ice cooled cake.

MAYONNAISE CHOCOLATE CAKE

1 cup mayonnaise, whipped
1 cup cold water
1 teaspoon vanilla
2 cups flour
1 cup sugar
4 Tablespoons cocoa
1½ teaspoons soda
dash of salt

Add water and vanilla to whipped mayonnaise and set aside. Sift dry ingredients together and add to mayonnaise mixture. Beat well. Bake at 350° in two 9 inch cake pans until done.

OOEY GOOEY BUTTER CAKE

1 yellow butter cake mix
1 egg
1 stick butter
2 eggs
1 box powdered sugar
1 8-oz. package cream cheese
1/2 cup chopped nuts

Mix first three ingredients and press into 9X13 buttered pan. Combine next three ingredients and pour over crust. Sprinkle top with chopped nuts and bake at 350° for 35-40 minutes. (Have butter and cream cheese at room temperature).

PINEAPPLE UPSIDE–DOWN CAKE

1 cup sugar
1/2 cup shortening
1 egg, beaten
1 cup milk
1/4 teaspoon salt
2 cups flour
2 teaspoons baking powder
3 Tablespoons butter
1 cup brown sugar
1 small can pineapple rings
1 jar cherries

Cream together sugar and shortening. Add egg, milk, and salt. Sift flour and baking powder together three times and add to above mixture beating well. Put butter in medium-sized iron skillet and melt. Sift brown sugar evenly over melted butter (do not stir), Take pineapple slices and place side by side over brown sugar and place a cherry in the center of each pineapple slice. Pour batter over this and bake at 350° for about 45 minutes. When done invert on plate. You may or may not want to top with sauce.

SAUCE

Leave 1/3 cup cake batter in pan, add 1 cup sugar, 1/2 cup butter and pineapple juice drained from slices. Cook until slightly thick. Add a dash of cinnamon.

168

PINEAPPLE CAKE

2 cups sugar
2 cups flour
1 teaspoon soda
1 cup chopped nuts
1 (303) can crushed pineapple, not drained
3 eggs, beaten

Mix all ingredients and pour into 9X13 greased and floured pan. Bake at 325° for 40 minutes. Ice while hot.

PINEAPPLE CAKE ICING

1 8-oz. package cream cheese
1 stick oleo
1 teaspoon vanilla
2 cups powdered sugar

Mix thoroughly and put on cake as soon as it comes from oven. Cover cake and let cool.

YELLOW LAYER CAKE

1/2 cup butter
1 cup sugar
1 cup milk
2 cups flour
2 eggs
2 teaspoons baking powder
dash of salt
1 teaspoon vanilla

Cream butter and sugar, add eggs and beat until light and creamy. Sift remaining dry ingredients and add to mixture along with milk amd vanilla, Stir until smooth. Bake in 350° oven until toothpick inserted in center comes out clean. Makes two layers.

169

PINEAPPLE CAKE

1 box pineapple cake mix
1 box coconut cream instant pudding
2/3 cup oil
3 eggs
1 10-oz. bottle carbonated lemon-lime soda

Mix together and bake in greased and floured sheet cake pan at 350° for 30-35 minutes. Ice as follows:

ICING

1 cup sugar
2 Tablespoons cornstarch
1 stick oleo
1 medium can crushed pineapple, drained
1 can flaked coconut
1 cup chopped nuts

Combine first four ingredients in saucepan and cook for 5 minutes. Stir in coconut and nuts while still cooking. Remove from stove and pour over hot cake.

YELLOW CAKE

2 cups flour
1-3/4 cups sugar
4 eggs
1/2 cup butter
1/2 cup shortening
1 cup buttermilk
3 teaspoons vanilla

Cream together sugar, butter, shortening, and eggs. Add flour and buttermilk. Add vanilla last. Pour into two 8 inch round cake pans that have been greased and floured. Bake at 325° until done.

CHOCOLATE POUND CAKE

1 white cake mix
4 eggs
3/4 cup oil
1 Tablespoon cocoa
3/4 cup water
1 package instant chocolate pudding
1 teaspoon vanilla

Mix all ingredients well with electric mixer. Pour in greased and floured loaf or bundt pan. Bake at 350° for 45 minutes.

GLAZE

2 cups powdered sugar
2 Tablespoons butter
1 teaspoon cocoa
1/3 cup water
1 teaspoon vanilla

Mix together and bring to a boil Punch holes in cake and pour glaze over while hot. Bake 5 more minutes.

RED VELVET CAKE

2¼ cups sugar
3/4 cup shortening
2 eggs
6 teaspoons cocoa
3 Tablespoons red food coloring
3 Tablespoons strong hot coffee
3 cups flour
1/2 teaspoon salt
1½ teaspoons soda
1½ cups buttermilk
1½ teaspoons vanilla

Cream sugar, shortening and eggs. Make a paste with coffee, coloring, and cocoa and add to mixture. Sift dry ingredients (except soda); mix soda, buttermilk, and vanilla. Add these to mixture alternately. Bake in 3 greased and floured round cake pans at 350° until done. Let cool and ice as follows:

ICING

2 sticks butter
1 cup sugar
1 cup milk
1 Tablespoon flour
1 teaspoon vanilla

Mix butter, sugar and vanilla. Cream at high speed on electric mixer for 7 minutes. Mix flour, milk and cook slowly, stirring constantly until thick. Cool. Beat into sugar and butter mixture and spread on cooled cake.

PRUNE CAKE

1 cup vegetable oil
1½ cups sugar
3 eggs, beaten
1 cup buttermilk
2 cups flour
1 teaspoon soda
1 teaspoon baking powder
1 teaspoon salt
1 cup nuts, chopped
1½ cups cooked prunes, chopped
1 teaspoon nutmeg
1 teaspoon vanilla

Combine ingredients in order given. Mix well after each. Bake in greased and floured layer pans at 350° until browned.

PRUNE CAKE FILLING

2 cups brown sugar
1 cup cream
1 Tablespoon butter
1/2 cup chopped nuts

Cook first three ingredients until it forms soft ball. Add nuts and pour over cake.

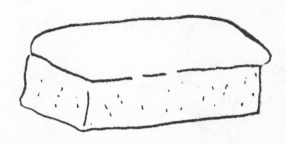

STRAWBERRY CAKE

1 box white cake mix
1 box strawberry gelatin, dry
1/2 cup oil
4 eggs
1/2 cup water
1/2 cup strawberries, crushed

Combine cake mix and gelatin. Add oil and water and beat until smooth. Add eggs one at a time, beating after each one. Add strawberries last. Bake 30-35 minutes at 350°. Can use either layer pans or 9X13.

ICING

1/2 stick oleo, melted
1 box powdered sugar
1/2 cup strawberries, crushed

Beat together until smooth and spread over cooled cake.

BEAT 'N EAT FROSTING

1 egg white
3/4 cup sugar
1/4 teaspoon cream of tarter
1 teaspoon vanilla
1/4 cup boiling water

Mix all ingredients together adding water last. Beat with electric mixer on high until stiff, and peaks are formed. Spread on cooled cake.

174

BUTTERSCOTCH ICING

1/2 cup milk
1 cup light brown sugar
1½ cups powdered sugar
5 Tablespoons butter
1 teaspoon vanilla

Combine milk, brown sugar and butter in heavy sauce pan. Boil 3 minutes, then cool. Add powdered sugar and vanilla. Beat until creamy and frost cake.

CARROT CAKE ICING

1 pound powdered sugar
1 stick butter, soft
1 8-oz. package cream cheese
1 teaspoon vanilla

Cream butter and cheese. Stir in sugar and vanilla. Blend well and spread on cake. Be sure butter and cheese are room temperature.

CHOCOLATE ICING

1 stick oleo, softened
4 cups powdered sugar
1/2 cup cocoa
1/2 cup evaporated milk
1/2 teaspoon vanilla

Mix well with electric mixer until thick and smooth.

CHOCOLATE SOUR CREAM FROSTING

1 12-oz. package semi-sweet chocolate chips
1/2 cup sour cream
2¼ cups powdered sugar
2½ Tablespoons milk

Melt chocolate chips in microwave or over double boiler. Do not heat more than just to melt. Let cool and add sour cream, sugar and milk beating until smooth. Add the milk only a little at a time, it may take a teaspoon more or less.

COFFEE ICING

3 cups powdered sugar
1 teaspoon vanilla
1/4 cup very strong black coffee
2 egg whites

Combine powdered sugar, coffee, and vanilla in saucepan and heat to lukewarm, stirring constantly. Beat egg whites until they form peaks and stir into other mixture. Ice cake while icing is warm.

DECORATOR ICING

2 pounds powdered sugar
1½ cups shortening
1/3 cup water
1 teaspoon butter flavoring

Beat until right consistency for decorator tube. Separate and use food colorings as desired.

LEMON GLAZE

1/4 cup butter
1/3 cup orange juice
1/2 cup lemon juice
3/4 cup sugar

Mix together in saucepan and cook over medium heat until butter is melted and mixture is blended and smooth. Cool slightly before pouring over cake. Yellow food coloring may be added to color. (Great on Lemon Bundt Cake).

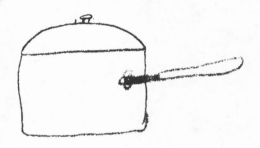

UNCOOKED WHITE FROSTING

2 egg whites
1/4 teaspoon salt
1/4 cup sugar
3/4 cup white corn syrup
1¼ teaspoons vanilla

Add salt to egg whites and beat with electric mixer until it forms soft peaks, gradually add sugar, beating constantly until smooth and glossy. Slowly add corn syrup until stiff peaks are formed. Add vanilla and beat in with spoon. Frost cool cake.

OTHER DESIRABLES

Pies and Pie Crusts

APPLE CRUNCH

1 quart raw apples, sliced
1 teaspoon cinnamon
2/3 cup sugar
1½ Tablespoons butter
1 cup flour
1/4 teaspoon cinnamon
1/2 cup brown sugar
1/2 cup butter

Place apples in oblong dish. Mix the 1 teaspoon cinnamon, sugar, and 1½ Tablespoons butter and sprinkle over apple slices. Blend flour, 1/4 teaspoon cinnamon and brown sugar. Cut in 1/2 cup softened butter until crumbly. Sprinkle topping over apples and bake at 375° about 1 hour. Any fruit may be used in place of apples.

APPLE PIE

5 cups apple slices
1/2 cup sugar
2 Tablespoons flour
1/2 teaspoon nutmeg
2 Tablespoons lemon juice

Put apples in unbaked crust. Mix remaining ingredients and pour over apples.

TOPPING: 1/2 cup sugar
          1/2 cup flour
          1 stick butter

Mix topping and sprinkle evenly on pie. Place in large brown paper bag, put on cookie sheet and bake at 425° for 1 hour on lower rack of oven.

180

BLACK BOTTOM PIE

16 gingersnaps, crushed
5 Tablespoons melted butter
2 cups scalded milk
1/2 cup sugar
4 egg yolks, well beaten
1½ Tablespoons cornstarch
1½ squares dark chocolate
1 teaspoon vanilla
1 Tablespoon unflavored gelatin
2 Tablespoons cold water
4 egg whites, beaten stiff
1/2 cup sugar
1/4 teaspoon cream of tarter
2 teaspoons bourbon
1 8-oz. carton frozen whipped topping

Mix gingersnaps and butter and press into 9 inch pie
pan. Bake at 375° for 10 minutes. Cool. For first
filling: Add egg yolks slowly to hot milk. Combine
sugar and cornstarch and stir into milk mixture. Cook
in double boiler for 20 minutes stirring occasionally
until it coats a spoon. Remove from heat and take out
1 cup of mixture, add chocolate to the cup of mixture
and beat as it cools. Add 1 teaspoon vanilla to
chocolate mixture, beat well and pour into pie crust.
Chill. For second filling: Dissolve gelatin in
water. Add to remaining custard and cool. Beat 1/2
cup sugar and cream of tarter into egg whites and beat
until sugar is dissolved. Add bourbon and fold into
custard mixture. Pour over chilled chocolate filling.
Cover top with frozen whipped topping. Shave dark
chocolate for garnish.

181

BUTTERMILK PIE

1½ cups sugar
3 Tablespoons flour
1 stick oleo
3 eggs
1 cup buttermilk
1 Tablespoon vanilla

Blend first four ingredients. Add milk and vanilla. Pour into unbaked pie shell and bake at 350° until done. (Approximately 50 minutes).

CANDY BAR PIE

1½ cups grated coconut
2 Tablespoons margarine
1 teaspoon instant coffee in 2 Tablespoons water
1½ 7½-oz. milk chocolate candy bars with almonds
4 cups frozen whipped topping

Mix coconut and margarine for crust and press into 8 inch pie plate and bake at 325° for 10 minutes. Cool. Combine coffee mixture and candy bars in double boiler until melted and very warm. Let cool and fold in whipped topping. Fill crust and shave other half of candy bars on top and freeze. Take out of freezer approximately 10 minutes before serving. Do not let this completely thaw or reach room temperature.

CHESS PIE

1½ cups sugar
1/2 cup milk
1 teaspoon vanilla
3/4 stick butter
2 eggs, beaten
2 Tablespoons flour

Mix flour with sugar. Add all other ingredients, mix thoroughly and put in unbaked pie crust. Bake at 350° for 45 minutes.

CHOCOLATE CREAM PIE

2 cups milk
1 cup sugar
1/2 cup flour
4 egg yolks
2 Tablespoons cocoa, heaping
1 teaspoon vanilla
dash of salt

Mix all ingredients except vanilla. Cook over medium heat stirring constantly until filling has thickened. Remove from heat and add vanilla. Beat well for just a minute to assure smoothness. Pour into baked pie crust and top with meringue. Bake at 350° until meringue is golden brown.

AUNT LOUIE'S CHOCOLATE PIE

6 egg yolks
1½ cups sugar
4 cups milk
5 Tablespoons cocoa
¾ cup flour
½ stick butter
2 teaspoons vanilla

Mix all ingredients together in a saucepan and cook over low to medium heat until thick. Pour into two baked pie shells and let cool. Top with meringue and bake at 350° until brown. Coconut may be substituted for chocolate.

JEFF DAVIS PIE

5 eggs
3 cups sugar
1/2 cup butter
1 teaspoon salt
1 teaspoon vanilla
1 large can evaporated milk

Mix all ingredients well and pour into two unbaked 9 inch pie crusts. Bake at 350° for about an hour.

MAMA'S JEFF DAVIS PIE

2 eggs
2 cups sugar
1/2 cup evaporated milk
2 Tablespoons flour
1/2 cup butter
1 teaspoon vanilla

Mix together in order given. Bake in an uncooked pie shell at 350° until pie is firm and will not shake in middle.

FAMOUS PIE

3/4 stick oleo, soft
1/2 box powdered sugar
3 egg yolks
1/4 teaspoon vanilla
1/2 pint whipping cream, whipped
3 Tablespoons powdered sugar
2/3 cup crushed pineapple, well drained
1/2 cup chopped pecans

Mix first four ingredients with mixer until light and fluffy. Pour in baked pie shell. Combine whipped cream and powdered sugar, fold in pineapple and nuts. Put on top of pie and refrigerate overnight.

LEMON PIE

1 cup sugar
3 Tablespoons cornstarch
1/4 cup butter
1/4 cup lemon juice
3 egg yolks
1 cup milk
1 carton sour cream

Combine sugar and cornstarch in pan. Add butter, juice and egg yolks. Stir in milk and cook over medium heat until thick. Cool. Fold in sour cream. Put in baked pie shell and top with meringue. Bake at 350° until lightly browned.

COCONUT CREAM PIE

2 cups milk
1 cup sugar
1/2 cup flour
4 egg yolks
1/2-3/4 cup coconut
1 teaspoon vanilla
dash of salt

Mix all ingredients together except coconut and vanilla. Cook over medium heat stirring constantly so as not to scorch. When filling starts to thicken add coconut and let cook until thick. Take off stove and add vanilla. Beat for a minute to help smoothness. Put in baked pie shell and top with meringue. Sprinkle top with coconut and bake at 350° until golden brown.

MAMA'S CUSTARD PIE

5 eggs, beaten until light and fluffy
2 cups milk
1 teaspoon vanilla
1 cup sugar
3 Tablespoons butter

Mix together and pour into pie crust. Sprinkle top with nutmeg. Cook 15 minutes at 400° then turn to 350° for 30 minutes. Start checking for doneness with toothpick in middle. This makes a big pie so build crust high around sides.

LEMON ICEBOX PIE

1 can sweetened condensed milk
1 Tablespoon sugar
2 egg yolks
juice of two lemons

Mix milk, sugar, and egg yolks well. Add lemon juice. Pour into graham cracker or vanilla wafer crust. Top with meringue and bake until golden brown at 350°.

PEANUT BUTTER CREAM PIE

1¼ cups vanilla wafer crumbs
1/4 cup sugar
6 Tablespoons butter, melted
1 8-oz. package cream cheese
1/2 cup peanut butter
1 cup powdered sugar
1/4 cup half and half
1 10-oz. carton frozen whipped topping

Combine first three ingredients, press in pie pan and chill. Beat together cream cheese and peanut butter until smooth. Add powdered sugar and half and half. Beat again until batter is smooth. Gently fold in whipped topping and blend well. Spoon into crust and chill thoroughly before serving.

PEANUT BUTTER PIE

3 eggs
1/2 cup sugar
1/2 cup peanut butter, crunchy
1 cup dark corn syrup
1 teaspoon vanilla

Mix with electric mixer on medium speed until well blended. Pour into unbaked pie shell and cook at 350° for 50-60 minutes. Crust will brown and pie filling will be fluffy. Cool completely before serving.

PECAN PIE

1/2 cup brown sugar
1/2 cup white sugar
1 heaping Tablespoon flour
3 eggs, beaten
1 cup whole pecans
1 cup light corn syrup
1 lump butter

Combine all ingredients and pour into unbaked pie shell. Bake at 375° for 45 minutes.

186

GRANDMA'S PECAN PIE

3 eggs
3 Tablespoons butter (scant)
1 teaspoon vanilla
1 cup sugar
1 cup white corn syrup
1 cup pecans
1 Tablespoon flour, heaping

Stir together, pour into unbaked pie crust, and bake for 10 minutes at 400°. Reduce to 350° and bake for 45 minutes more.

CONFUSED LEMON MERINGUE PIE

6 egg whites
pinch of salt
1½ cups sugar
3/8 teaspoon cream of tarter
2 boxes lemon pie filling
1 cup frozen whipped topping
1/2 cup powdered sugar

Beat egg whites and salt until foamy. Add cream of tarter and beat. Add sugar slowly continuing to beat until very stiff. Put in well buttered pie pan and bake for one hour at 250°. Cook pie filling per package directions. Let cool, add 1/2 cup whipped topping, & cover cooled meringue. Mix 1/2 cup whipped topping and powdered sugar and spread over lemon filling. Refrigerate.

PUMPKIN PIE

1½ cups cooked pumpkin
1 teaspoon salt
1 teaspoon cinnamon
1 teaspoon ginger
2 eggs, beaten
1½ cups milk
3 Tablespoons orange juice

Mix together and put in an unbaked pie crust. Bake at 350° for about 40 minutes.

187

PUMPKIN PIE

2 eggs, beaten
1 cup plus 1 teaspoon brown sugar, packed
1 Tablespoon flour
1/2 teaspoon allspice
1/2 teaspoon nutmeg
1 small can evaporated milk
1 cup pumpkin

Mix all ingredients together and bake in unbaked pie shell for 15 minutes at 350°, then for 45 minutes at 275°.

RHUBARB PIE

2 cups rhubarb
1 cup sugar
1 egg
2 Tablespoons flour
1 Tablespoon lemon juice
2 Tablespoons butter

Cut rhubarb into very small pieces without peeling. Sift sugar and flour together and add egg, mix with rhubarb and lemon juice. Put in unbaked pie shell and cover with pie crust. Bake at 450° for 10 minutes, reduce heat and bake at 350° for 30 minutes.

STRAWBERRY PIE

1 quart strawberries
1 cup sugar
2 teaspoons cornstarch
2 Tablespoons lemon juice

Divide berries in half, saving the choice berries for whole. Mash the others with potato masher and add sugar and cornstarch. Cook 5 minutes over medium heat until thickened. Add lemon juice and let cool. Place 1/2 whole berries evenly in baked pie shell. Pour mixture over all making sure all raw berries are covered. Top this with whipped topping. Refrigerate.

STRAWBERRY CHIFFON PIE

1 small package strawberry gelatin
1 cup hot water
1½ cups crushed sweetened strawberries
1/4 cup sugar
2 egg whites, beaten stiff
1/2 cup whipping cream, whipped

Dissolve gelatin in hot water. Chill until partially set. Beat fluffy and fold in berries. Gradually beat sugar into egg whites until dissolved. Gently fold egg whites and whipped cream into gelatin mixture. Pour into cooled baked pie shell. Chill until set. Top with whipped cream.

FROZEN STRAWBERRY PIE

2 egg whites
1 cup sugar
1 cup strawberries
1 pint whipping cream, whipped

Beat first three ingredients on high speed for 10 minutes. Fold in whipped cream. Put in graham cracker crumb pie shell and freeze.

VINEGAR PIE

3 egg yolks
1 cup sugar
4 Tablespoons flour
1/2 cup vinegar
2 cups boiling water
1 teaspoon lemon flavoring or juice

Mix egg yolks, sugar, flour with just enough cold water to mix. Add vinegar and boiling water. Cook over medium heat until thick. Add lemon flavoring or juice. Pour into baked pie shell and top with meringue.

189

ONE CUP COBBLER

1 stick oleo
1 cup flour
1 cup sugar
1 cup milk
2 teaspoons baking powder
1/4 teaspoon salt
fruit

Melt butter in 9X13 baking dish. Mix other ingredients except fruit and pour batter over melted butter. Place fruit evenly on top of batter and bake at 350° for one hour or until golden brown. (Batter will bake through and come to top).

EGG CUSTARD

4 eggs
3/4 cup sugar
1 Tablespoon flour
2 cups milk
1/4 teaspoon salt
2 Tablespoons butter
1/4 teaspoon nutmeg
1 teaspoon vanilla

Beat first three ingredients well, then add others. Pour into unbaked pie shell and bake at 450° for 10 minutes then 325° for 20 minutes.

PIE CRUST

3 cups flour
1 rounded cup shortening
7 Tablespoons water
1 egg, beaten
1 teaspoon vinegar
1/4 teaspoon salt

Blend flour and shortening with pastry blender until mealy. Add remaining ingredients. Work dough as little as possible to mix. Divide in three equal pieces, roll out and place in pie pan. This makes three crusts and can be frozen until ready to use.

STIR AND ROLL PIE CRUST

2 cups flour
1/2 cup oil
1/2 teaspoon salt
1/4 cup water or milk

Mix together and stir vigorously until flour mixture pulls away from sides of bowl. Do not work dough. Divide in half and roll between wax paper. Makes two crusts.

VANILLA WAFER OR GRAHAM CRACKER CRUST

1¼ cups crushed cookies or crackers
1/4 cup sugar
1/2 cup melted butter (slight)

Mix together and press in pie pan.

MERINGUE

egg whites
sugar
cream of tarter

Use one tablespoon sugar to one egg white, and 1/8 teaspoon cream of tarter to three egg whites. Beat egg whites until they are stiff. Add sugar and cream of tarter while beating.

PECAN TARTS

CRUST: 3 oz. cream cheese
         1 stick butter
         1 cup flour

Mix together, form into small balls and press into miniature muffin pans.

FILLING: 2 Tablespoons light corn syrup
           1 cup light brown sugar
           2 Tablespoons butter
           1 teaspoon vanilla
           2/3 cup chopped pecans

Mix together and fill each little crust. Bake at 350° for 20 minutes. These are great for Christmas baking.

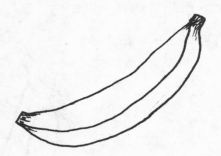

VANILLA OR BANANA PUDDING

1 cup evaporated milk
1 cup whole milk
1 cup sugar
1/4 cup flour
3 eggs yolks
1 teaspoon vanilla
vanilla wafers for crust

Mix flour and sugar. Add remaining ingredients and cook on low temperature until thickens. For banana pudding, slice 2 large bananas and add just as you take off stove. Line dish with whole vanilla wafers and pour pudding mixture over. Crumble vanilla wafers on top or make meringue from egg whites.

OTHER DESIRABLES

OTHER DESIRABLES

Cookies

MAMA'S TEA CAKES

½ cup butter
1½ cups sugar
3 eggs
1 teaspoon baking powder
1 teaspoon vanilla
1 cup flour

Mix all ingredients in order given. Add additional flour to make a stiff dough. Roll on floured board about 1/4-inch thick and cut with cookie cutter. Bake at 350° until cookies just start to turn color. Do not let them brown or they will be overbaked.

MERINGUE COOKIES

2 egg whites
1 cup nuts
1/2 cup sugar
1 teaspoon vanilla
1/4 teaspoon salt

Beat egg whites and salt until stiff. Slowly add sugar beating constantly until peaks form. Add vanilla (still mixing), then gently fold in chopped nuts with spoon. Drop on buttered cookie sheet and bake at 250° for 40 minutes.

JAM/JELLY COOKIES

2¼ cups sifted flour
8 Tablespoons sugar
1 teaspoon vanilla
1/2 cup ground nuts
1 cup oleo
jams/jellies-optional flavors

Soften butter or oleo before using. Cream sugar and butter thoroughly, then gradually add vanilla, nuts and flour. Roll into tiny balls in palm of hands. Make small depression in center of balls and fill with jam or jelly. Bake at 325° for approximately 15 minutes or until light brown.

DISHPAN COOKIES

2 cups light brown sugar
2 cups white sugar
2 teaspoons vanilla
2 cups oil
4 eggs
4 cups flour
2 teaspoons soda
1 teaspoon salt
1½ cups quick-cooking oats
4 cups corn flakes

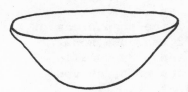

Cream first 5 ingredients together well. Add flour, soda and salt. Fold in oats and corn flakes. Drop from spoon onto cookie sheet and bake at 350° for 7-8 minutes. Do not overbake; these are better soft.

LEMON GINGER COOKIES

2½ cups flour
2 teaspoons baking soda
1 teaspoon cinnamon
1/4 teaspoon salt
3 teaspoons ginger
3/4 cup butter
1 cup dark brown sugar, packed
1 egg
1/4 cup molasses
1/4 cup sugar
1 Tablespoon ground lemon rind

Beat butter, brown sugar, and egg until light and fluffy, add molasses and lemon rind and beat until well blended. Sift dry ingredients twice and add a little at a time to butter mixture. Roll dough into balls (1 Tablespoon), roll in granulated sugar and place 2 inches apart on ungreased cookie sheet. Bake at 350° for 10 minutes. Cookies should be soft in center. Cool completely separated. Do not stack hot.

197

ICEBOX COOKIES

1 cup brown sugar
3/4 cup butter
1 egg
1/2 teaspoon cream of tarter
1/2 teaspoon soda
1 teaspoon vanilla
1 cup nuts, chopped
flour

Mix well in order given. Add enough flour to make stiff dough. Roll in approximately 12-inch rolls about 1½-inches thick. Chill. Slice thin and bake at 350° for 12 to 15 minutes. These may be frozen then cut and baked.

PINWHEEL COOKIES

COOKIE DOUGH:
1 cup brown sugar
1 cup white sugar
1 cup shortening
3 eggs
4 cups flour
1/2 teaspoon salt
1 teaspoon soda

Cream together sugar and shortening, add eggs one at a time. Sift together all dry ingredients and mix with sugar. Divide dough and roll out each half 1/4-inch thick, spread with date mixture and roll up jelly roll style. Must be thoroughly chilled overnight before cooking. Slice 1/4-inch thick and bake at 350° until brown.

DATE FILLING:
1 pound chopped dates
1/2 cup water
1 cup sugar
1 cup chopped nuts
1/2 teaspoon lemon juice

Bring dates, water and sugar to a boil. Remove from stove and add nuts and lemon juice. Let cool before spreading on dough.

198

PEANUT BUTTER COOKIES

1 cup shortening
1 cup white sugar
1 cup brown sugar
2 eggs
3 cups flour
1½ teaspoons soda
1/4 teaspoon salt
1 teaspoon vanilla
1 cup peanut butter

Cream shortening and sugar. Add eggs and vanilla.
Sift together flour, salt, and soda and add to
mixture. Add peanut butter last. Mix thoroughly and
roll into 3/4-inch balls. Place 1 inch apart on
cookie sheet and press with fork twice to make
criss-cross.

NO BAKE CHOCOLATE OATMEAL COOKIES

2 cups sugar
1/2 cup milk
4 Tablespoons cocoa
1 stick butter
1/2 cup peanut butter
1 teaspoon vanilla
3 cups quick cooking oats

Cook sugar, milk, cocoa, and butter over medium heat
to soft ball stage. Stir in peanut butter, vanilla,
and oatmeal. Drop on wax paper from spoon.

RICE CRISPY CRUNCH

1 cup sugar
6 cups popped rice cereal
1 cup peanut butter
1 cup light corn syrup
1½ cups semi-sweet chocolate chips

Bring sugar and syrup to a boil. Take off heat and
add peanut butter and cereal. Press into 9X13 inch
buttered pan. Melt chocolate and spread over top.
Cool and cut.

RAISIN OATMEAL COOKIES

1 cup raisins
2¼ cups flour
1 teaspoon salt
1/2 teaspoon soda
1½ teaspoons cinnamon
1/2 teaspoon nutmeg
1 cup soft shortening
1½ cups firmly packed brown sugar
1 egg
1 Tablespoon water
2 cups quick cooking oats

Let raisins stand in boiling water for 10 minutes; drain. Mix dry ingredients, add eggs, water, and shortening and beat two minutes. Stir in oats and raisins and chill. Roll only 1/4 dough at a time on floured board to 1/4 inch thickness. Cut with cookie cutter and bake at 375° for 10-12 minutes.

SNICKERDOODLES

1 cup shortening
1½ cups sugar
2 eggs
2-3/4 cups flour
2 teaspoons cream of tarter
1 teaspoon baking soda
1/4 teaspoon salt
2 Tablespoons sugar
1½ teaspoons cinnamon

Mix thoroughly first three ingredients, then add next four ingredients in order. In separate bowl, mix sugar and cinnamon. Roll into 1-inch balls and roll in sugar and cinnamon mixture. Place 2 inches apart on ungreased cookie sheet and bake at 400° for 8-10 minutes.

GINGERSNAPS

2 cups molasses
1 cup shortening
1/4 teaspoon salt
2 Tablespoons soda
1 teaspoon ground ginger
flour

Boil molasses and shortening. Add all ingredients except flour and mix. Add enough flour to make dough. Roll thin, cut and bake at 350° until done.

PECAN MELTS

1 cup flour
1/2 cup soft butter
4 Tablespoons powdered sugar
1/2 cup finely chopped pecans

Mix ingredients in order given, mixing well after each. Form into balls or oblong rolls. Bake at 350° until light brown. Sprinkle with powdered sugar while hot.

SPRITZ COOKIES

1 cup sugar
1 cup butter
1 egg
2 cups flour
1 teaspoon almond flavoring

Cream together butter and sugar. Blend in egg and add flour and flavoring. Mix well. Put dough through cookie press and bake at 400° for 10-12 minutes.

COOKIE FROSTING

1 egg
1/4 teaspoon cream of tarter
1¼ cups powdered sugar

Beat egg and cream of tarter until frothy. Gradually beat in sugar until thick and glossy. Food coloring may be added if desired.

201

RACHEL'S LITTLE WHITE COOKIES

2 sticks oleo
2 Tablespoons powdered sugar
2 cups flour
1 teaspoon vanilla
2 cups chopped nuts

Cream butter and sugar. Add flour and other ingredients. Shape in balls about the size of a walnut and place on ungreased cookie sheet. Bake at 325° for 15 to 20 minutes. Roll in powdered sugar while warm.

OTHER DESIRABLES

OTHER DESIRABLES

Candy

ALMOND COCONUT CANDY

2 boxes powdered sugar
1 stick butter
1 can sweetened condensed milk
1 14-oz. package coconut
3/4 cup paraffin
1 12-oz. package semi-sweet chocolate chips
whole roasted almonds

Mix first four ingredients and make into 1X2 inch rectangles, then lightly press whole almond into center of each. Melt paraffin and chocolate in top of double boiler. Dip bars, almond side up, holding with toothpicks on both sides. Tilt sideways to let chocolate run off and set on waxed paper.

CHOCOLATE DIPPED COCONUT BALLS

1 box powdered sugar
1 stick butter, melted
1 cup coconut
2 teaspoons milk
1 teaspoon vanilla
1 12-oz. package semi-sweet chocolate pieces
1 block paraffin

Melt chocolate and paraffin in top of double boiler. Combine remaining ingredients and roll into balls. Dip balls in warm chocolate and paraffin mixture, and place on waxed paper.

CHOCOLATE DIPPED PEANUT BUTTER BALLS

1½ cups peanut butter
2/3 cup butter, softened
1 teaspoon vanilla
1 box powdered sugar
1 12-oz. package semi-sweet chocolate pieces
1/4 cup paraffin (scant)

Mix together first 3 ingredients, then slowly blend in sugar. Roll into 3/4 inch balls. Melt chocolate pieces and paraffin in microwave or in top of double boiler. Dip balls in chocolate mixture and place on waxed paper.

CHOCOLATE DIPPED UNCOOKED CANDY

1 can sweetened condensed milk
1 can flaked coconut
1 quart chopped pecans
1 stick butter
1-3/4 boxes powdered sugar

Melt butter, pour over pecans, and let stand while mixing other ingredients. After mixing other ingredients add pecans and shape into small balls and refrigerate overnight. Melt 1 stick paraffin and 24 ounces chocolate chips in top of double boiler. Keep this hot while dipping. Place balls on waxed paper after dipping. Makes 100-125.

TAFFY

3 cups sugar
1 cup light corn syrup
1/2 cup vinegar
1/2 cup dark corn syrup

Cook slowly in iron skillet until hard ball forms in cold water. Pour into two buttered dishes. When cool, butter hands well and pull. Pull straight; do not twist. When hardens, break into small pieces.

TOO MARVELOUS MARSHMALLOW FUDGE

2¼ cups sugar
3/4 cup evaporated milk
1/4 cup butter
1 5-oz. jar marshmallow cream
1 6-oz. package semi-sweet chocolate chips
3/4 cup pecans, chopped
1 teaspoon vanilla

Combine first four ingredients and cook to boiling point over medium to high heat. Boil 4 minutes stirring constantly. (Will be caramel colored at this point). Remove from heat and add chocolate, nuts, and vanilla. Stir until chocolate is melted and fudge begins to hold a shape. Pour in buttered 9 inch square pan and cool.

DIVINITY

4 cups sugar
1 cup water
1 teaspoon vanilla
1 cup light corn syrup
3 egg whites, beaten stiff
2 cups nuts, chopped

Cook sugar, syrup, and water to hard ball stage. Add gradually to egg whites and beat well. Add vanilla and nuts. Drop by teaspoon on waxed paper.

NEVER FAIL DIVINITY

2 cups sugar
1/2 cup water
1 pint marshmallow cream
1/2 cup nuts, chopped
1 teaspoon vanilla

Boil sugar and water until hard ball forms in cold water. Pour mixture over marshmallow cream stirring until slightly cool. Fold in nuts and vanilla. Drop by spoon onto waxed paper.

DIVINITY

2 cups sugar
1/2 cup hot water
1/2 cup light corn syrup
2 egg whites, beaten
1 cup chopped pecans
1 teaspoon vanilla

Cook sugar, water and corn syrup until hard ball forms in cold water. Pour over egg whites slowly beating continuously. Add nuts and vanilla and beat until ready to pour into buttered pyrex dish. Let set and cut into squares.

PEANUT BARS

1/2 cup granulated sugar
1/2 cup brown sugar
1 cup light corn syrup
1 cup peanuts with husks
1 cup peanut butter
6 cups corn flakes
1 12-oz. package milk chocolate chips

Combine first three ingredients in sauce pan and bring to a boil. Add remaining ingredients except chocolate chips and mix well. Press into a buttered 9X13 pan and cover with melted chocolate chips.

PEANUT BUTTER CHEWYS

1 cup sugar
1 cup white corn syrup
1 cup peanut butter
8 cups corn flakes

Bring sugar and syrup to a boil. Take off stove immediately and add peanut butter. Stir until melted. Pour over corn flakes in another bowl and stir to coat. Spoon onto waxed paper.

PEANUT BRITTLE

3 cups sugar
1-1/8 cups white corn syrup
1/2 cup water
4 cups raw peanuts
3 teaspoons butter
1 teaspoon vanilla
2½ teaspoons soda

Boil sugar, syrup, and water until it reaches 250° on candy thermometer. Add peanuts and stir continuously until temperature reaches 290°. Remove from heat, add butter, vanilla, and soda. Pour on buttered cookie sheets or candy board and spread as thin as possible. Let cool and break into pieces.

PEANUT BUTTER CUPS

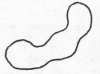

2 large chocolate bars
1 stick paraffin
1½ cups peanut butter
2 sticks butter
1 box powdered sugar

Melt one chocolate bar in top of double boiler with 1/2 stick paraffin. Pour into buttered 9X13 pan. Mix peanut butter, butter and sugar together. Make second layer in pan over chocolate. Melt the other chocolate bar and paraffin and pour over peanut butter layer. Chill and cut into squares.

PEANUT BUTTER DIVINITY

2 cups sugar
2/3 cup milk
1 cup crunchy peanut butter
1 pint jar marshmallow cream

Cook sugar and milk to soft ball stage. Add peanut butter and marshmallow cream and stir until melted. Pour into square buttered pan. Cut as desired when cool.

PEANUT BUTTER GEMS

2 cups semi-sweet chocolate pieces
1 cup crunchy peanut butter
1½ cups graham cracker crumbs
1 cup butter, melted
3/4 pound powdered sugar

Melt chocolate and keep warm. Mix other ingredients and pat into 9X13 pan. Spread melted chocolate on top. Chill and cut into squares.

SUGAR PEANUTS

1 cup sugar
1/2 cup water
2 cups raw peanuts
salt

Cook sugar, water and peanuts in iron skillet until all moisture is absorbed and peanuts are sugar coated. Spread on cookie sheet, lightly salt and bake at 350° for 15 minutes. Stir and salt again lightly. Return to oven and cook another 15 minutes.

PEANUT SUGAR PATTIES

2½ cups sugar
2/3 cup light corn syrup
1 cup milk
4 teaspoons butter
1 cup powdered sugar
4 drops red food coloring
1½ cups raw peanuts

Cook sugar, syrup, milk and peanuts one hour on low heat or until soft ball stage. Add butter, food coloring, and powdered sugar. Beat until thickens and drop into patties on waxed paper.

JEAN'S PRALINES

1 box butterscotch pudding mix (not instant)
1/2 cup brown sugar
1 cup white sugar
1 Tablespoon butter
1/2 cup evaporated milk
1 cup pecans

Cook all ingredients together, except pecans, to soft ball stage. Add pecans and beat until mixture starts to thicken. Drop on waxed paper.

SUPER PRALINES

3 cups white sugar
1/2 cup light corn syrup
1/2 cup evaporated milk
pinch of salt
1/4 pound butter
1/2 teaspoon vanilla
pecans

Combine first four ingredients and cook slowly, stirring constantly until mixture forms firm ball in cold water. Remove from stove and add butter and vanilla. Cool a short while and beat. Then add pecans as desired. Drop on waxed paper.

CARAMEL PECAN CLUSTERS

1 14-oz. package caramels
2 Tablespoons evaporated milk
1 6-oz. package semi-sweet chocolate chips
1 cup pecans
1/4 block paraffin

Melt caramels and milk in top of double boiler. Add pecans and mix well. Drop on cookie sheet and let cool. Melt chocolate pieces and paraffin in top of double boiler. Dip candy in chocolate and recool.

OTHER DESIRABLES

OTHER DESIRABLES

Beverages

CHOCOLATE COFFEE MIX

2 cups hot cocoa mix
2 cups non-dairy creamer
1½ cups instant decaffeinated coffee
1½ cups powdered sugar
1/2 teaspoon cinnamon
1/2 teaspoon nutmeg

Mix together well and store in very tight container.
Combine 3 or 4 teaspoons mix to 1 cup hot water.

HOT CHOCOLATE FOR A CROWD

3 gallons water
3 cups cocoa
3 cups sugar
1½ teaspoons salt
3 pounds non-fat dry milk
1 Tablespoon vanilla

Heat 1-3/4 gallons water in large kettle. Mix cocoa,
sugar and salt. Dip out a small amount of water and
mix with dry ingredients, blending well. Add to water
and boil for 5 minutes. Add dry milk to 1-1/4 gallons
water. Beat with whip until smooth. Add to cooked
cocoa and heat to boiling. Add vanilla just before
serving.

INSTANT COCOA MIX

8 quart box non-fat dry milk
1 pound box cocoa mix
1 11-oz. jar non-dairy creamer
1/2 cup powdered sugar
2 Tablespoons cocoa

Mix together and store. To make hot chocolate, use
1/3 cup mix in mug and fill with boiling water.

216

BIRTHDAY PARTY PUNCH

3 packages unsweetened raspberry soft drink mix
1 large can pineapple juice
2 cans water
2 cups sugar
2 16-oz. bottles carbonated lemon-lime soft drink

Mix all ingredients well. Add carbonated soda just before serving.

COFFEE PUNCH

1 pint milk
2 quarts strong coffee, cooled
1 Tablespoon vanilla, scant
1/2 cup sugar
1 carton whipping cream
1/2 gallon ice cream

Mix together milk, coffee, vanilla and sugar. Chill. Place ice cream in punch bowl and pour mixture over. Cover with whipped cream and sprinkle with nutmeg.

FRUIT PUNCH

1 quart tea
1 quart cranberry juice
1 quart orange juice
1 pint lemonade
1 pint grape juice
1 pint pineapple juice
2 quarts ginger ale

Mix together, chill and serve.

JUST PLAIN PUNCH

1-3/4 cups sugar
1½ cups lemon juice
1/2 cup orange juice
2 cups grape juice
3 cups tea
1 quart ginger ale

Mix all ingredients, except ginger ale, and bring to a boil. Let cool to room temperature then refrigerate. When ready to serve, add 1 quart chilled ginger ale.

PINEAPPLE PUNCH

1 small package orange-pineapple flavored gelatin
2 small packages lemon flavored gelatin
9 cups boiling water
1 can crushed pineapple, not drained
4 cups sugar
4 cups water
1 16-oz. bottle concentrated lemon juice
2 46-oz. cans pineapple juice
4 quarts ginger ale

Dissolve gelatin in boiling water and add pineapple. Combine sugar and 4 cups water and bring to a boil. Stir into gelatin mixture and let cool. Add lemon and pineapple juice. Put into half gallon milk cartons and freeze. Makes 3½ cartons. Take out of freezer about 1 hour before serving, add 1 bottle ginger ale to each carton of punch. Serve this as a slush.

PUNCH

2 small cans frozen orange juice
2 packages strawberry soft drink mix, unsweetened
1 large can pineapple juice

Mix soft drink mix according to package directions and add other ingredients. Mix well, chill and serve.

SCHOOL DAY PUNCH

1 small package unsweetened soft drink mix
1 cup sugar
1 quart water
1 small can pineapple juice
1 quart ginger ale

Mix all ingredients except ginger ale and chill thoroughly. Put in freezer until slushy, take from freezer, add chilled ginger ale and serve. Colors: cherry mix for pink, lime for green, ½ lemon and ½ orange for yellow, and raspberry for red.

SHERBET PUNCH

2 small cans frozen orange juice
4 small cans frozen lemonade
4 small cans frozen pineapple juice
1 32-oz. bottle carbonated lemon-lime soft drink
1 gallon pineapple sherbet

Mix all juices as directed on cans, then mix together. When ready to serve, put sherbet in punch bowl and pour fruit mixture over sherbet. Add soft drink to taste.

SMOKED PUNCH

1 piece dry ice
1 quart ginger ale
1 quart club soda
2 46-oz. cans pineapple juice
1 small can frozen lemonade
1 small can frozen limeade
1 package frozen strawberries, crushed

Place dry ice in bottom of punch bowl. Mix all ingredients together and pour over dry ice into punch bowl.

219

INSTANT SPICED TEA MIX

2 cups powdered orange breakfast drink mix
1 cup instant tea
1 cup sugar
1 package lemonade mix with sugar
1 teaspoon powdered cloves
1 teaspoon cinnamon

Mix together and store in tightly closed container.
To serve: Add 1 teaspoon mix to 1 cup hot water.

SPICED TEA

1 small can frozen orange juice
1 small can frozen lemonade
3 cups strong brewed tea
2 quarts water
2 cups sugar
4 sticks cinnamon
8 whole cloves

Boil water and sugar. Remove from stove, add cinnamon
and cloves and steep. Mix juices and tea together and
add to water mixture.

SPICED TEA

1 small can frozen orange juice
1 small can frozen lemonade
1 quart apple juice
1 cup sugar
1½ teaspoons cloves
2 sticks cinnamon
1 teaspoon ginger
5 cups boiling water
3 cups strong brewed tea

Mix juices together. Place over low heat and add
spices and sugar. When this mixture becomes very
warm, pour in boiling water and tea. Steep. Do not
boil.

220

BLOODY MARYS

1 46-oz. can tomato juice
1 teaspoon salt
1½ teaspoons celery salt
1/2 teaspoon pepper
1/2 teaspoon hot sauce
4 Tablespoons Worcestershire sauce
juice of 3 lemons
2 cups vodka (optional)

Mix all ingredients except vodka and refrigerate. Pour into glasses when chilled and add vodka as desired.

BRANDY ICE

2 cups real vanilla ice cream
5 ounces brandy

Mix in blender until smooth. A little milk may be added to soften for blender. Serve immediately. Can be put in the freezer for approximately 45 minutes.

CHOCOLATE MINT SHAKE

1 quart vanilla ice cream
1/2 cup milk
1/3 cup chocolate mint liqueur

Put all ingredients in blender and mix only until blended. Mixture should be thick enough to eat with a spoon.

221

EGGNOG

1 pint whipping cream, whipped
12 eggs, separated
3/4 cup sugar
1/2 gallon vanilla ice cream, softened
bourbon to taste
nutmeg

Beat egg whites until they form a peak. Fold together with whipped cream. Beat egg yolks in separate dish, slowly adding sugar. Gradually beat in egg whites and whipped cream. Add ice cream last, beating well. Add bourbon to individual glasses, pour in eggnog and top with nutmeg.

FROZEN MARGARITAS

1 small can frozen limeade
1 limeade can tequila
3/4 limeade can triple sec
crushed ice

Put ingredients in blender, adding ice until slushy. Cover bottom of saucer with lime juice. Cover bottom of second saucer with salt. Set rim of glass in lime juice, then in salt. Fill glasses with margaritas.

FROZEN STRAWBERRY DAIQUIRIS

1 cup fresh or frozen strawberries
1 small can frozen limeade
1 limeade can light rum

Put all in blender and mix. Add ice until thick and slushy.

222

HOLIDAY EGGNOG

6 eggs
1 cup sugar
1 quart half and half
1 quart golden rum
nutmeg

Beat eggs in large mixing bowl until light and frothy.
Add sugar and beat until thick and lemon colored.
Stir in rum and slowly add cream beating constantly.
Chill several hours. Sprinkle with nutmeg when
served.

HOT BUTTERED RUM

1/2 gallon apple cider
1/2 cup brown sugar
1/2 stick butter
1/4 teaspoon cinnamon

Boil cider, sugar and cinnamon. Add butter. Pour
1-oz. rum into mug and fill with hot cider mixture.
This can be refrigerated, reheated and served.

IRISH COFFEE

1 oz. Irish whiskey
1 teaspoon sugar
1 Tablespoon whipped cream
black perked coffee

Pour whiskey into large coffee mug. Fill to within 1
inch of top with coffee. Add sugar, stir to dissolve
and top with a dollop of whipped cream. Let whipped
cream float; do not stir.

MARY'S CANARIES

1/2 cup galliano
1/4 cup creme de banana
1/4 cup kahlua
1 cup rum
2 cups pineapple juice
4 cups orange juice

Mix together well in 1/2 gallon container.

MINT JULEP

4 mint leaves
1 teaspoon sugar
1 teaspoon water
2 ounces bourbon
lemon wedges
crushed ice

Mix mint leaves, sugar and water. Pour into chilled glass. Fill with crushed ice and pour in 1 ounce bourbon. Stir for a minute or two until the ice melts down a couple of inches. Fill back up with ice and pour in remaining bourbon. Stir again. Squeeze lemon wedge and cut one for edge. of .glass.

WINE COOLERS

heavy dark red wine
carbonated lemon-lime soft drink

Mix wine coolers 2 parts wine to 1 part soft drink. Can be mixed half and half.

OTHER DESIRABLES

OTHER DESIRABLES

Pickles and Relishes

ROSE'S BREAD AND BUTTER PICKLES

20 medium size cucumbers, washed and cut crosswise in 1/8th inch slices. 10 peeled and sliced medium white onions. 3 bell peppers cut into fine shreds, after removing stems and seeds. Mix 3/4 cup non-iodized salt with the vegetables and put 1 quart crushed ice on top. Cover with weighted plate and let stand 3 hours. Drain. Make syrup of: 5 cups vinegar, 5 cups sugar, 2 Tablespoons white mustard seed, and 1 teaspoon each: tumeric powder, celery seed, and whole pepper seeds. Bring to boiling point, but DO NOT BOIL. Add vegetables and again bring to boiling point, but DO NOT BOIL. Seal immediately in hot, sterile jars.

CINNAMON PICKLES

Peel and cut into 1/4 inch slices, 2 gallons of overgrown cucumbers that are turning yellow. Cut seeds from middle, leaving rings. Soak 24 hours in 2 cups pickling lime and 2 gallons water. Rinse well and soak 3 hours in ice water. Put on stove and simmer 2 hours in 1 Tablespoon alum, 3 oz. red food coloring, 1 cup vinegar, and just enough water to cover. Drain. Bring to a boil the following: 3 cups vinegar, 3 cups water, 15 cups sugar, 12 whole sticks cinnamon, and 2 packages red hots. Pour this mixture over cucumbers and let set 24 hours. Drain liquid into saucepan, reheat to boiling, pour over cucumbers and let set another 24 hours. Repeat the third time. Pack rings in sterile jars, heat liquid again and pour over rings in jars. Seal.

DILL PICKLES

6 cups vinegar
2 cups water
1 cup canning salt
1 stem dill, with seeds, per jar
small cucumbers

Place dill and cucumbers in sterile pint jars. Boil liquid and salt and pour over cucumbers and seal.

LIME PICKLES

FIRST DAY: 7 pounds cucumbers cut 1/4 inch thick, covered with 2 gallons water and 2 cups pickling lime. Soak for 24 hours in enamel pot or crock.

SECOND DAY: Drain cucumbers and rinse well. Soak 3 hours in ice water, drain, cover with the following solution: 2 quarts pure apple cider vinegar, 4½ pounds sugar, 1 tablespoon salt, 1 teaspoon each:cloves, celery seed, and pickling spices. Heat, pour over cucumbers, and let set overnight.

THIRD DAY: Cook all for 40 minutes, pack in sterile jars and seal.

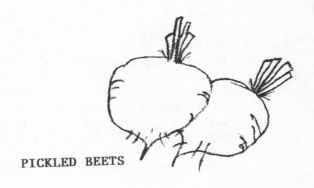

PICKLED BEETS

beets
water
sugar
vinegar

Wash beets leaving roots on and remove tops to within one to two inches of beets. Cover with water and cook until tender. (This varies with size of beet). Remove from heat, cut off tops and roots and peel. Mix together equal parts vinegar and sugar, put sliced or quartered beets in mixture and heat until beets are hot all the way through. Place beets in sterile jars, add juice to cover and seal.

PICKLED EGGS

8 hard boiled eggs
2 cups vinegar
1/2 teaspoon salt
1/4 teaspoon pepper
1/2 teaspoon dry mustard

Peel eggs and place in sterile jar. Heat vinegar and spices to boiling. Pour into jar over eggs, put on lid and let eggs set for 2 weeks before eating. Do not have to seal.

PICKLED OKRA

2 pounds small okra
4 Tablespoons dill seed
4 cloves garlic
3 cups vinegar
1½ cups water
1/2 cup salt

Pack okra in sterile pint jars. Add 1 Tablespoon dill seed and 1 clove garlic to each jar. Mix vinegar, water and salt. Heat to boiling point and pour over okra in jars and seal. Do not use for 1 month. Chill before serving.

PICKLED TOMATOES

1 gallon small green tomatoes, quartered
1 quart chopped onions
3/4 cup hot green peppers, chopped
1½ quarts vinegar
1/2 cup salt

Heat all ingredients together. Just at boiling point, fill jars and seal. Process in hot water bath 5 full minutes. Do not use for 3 weeks.

SQUASH PICKLES

1 gallon small sliced yellow squash
1½ cups bell pepper, cut in thin strips
4 cups onions, diced
1 clove garlic, chopped
1 hot pepper, chopped
1 jar pimentos, chopped
2/3 cup non-iodized salt
4 cups cider vinegar
3½ cups sugar
1 teaspoon each: celery seed, mustard seed, tumeric powder

Place squash, bell pepper, onion, garlic, hot pepper, and pimento in large pan. Cover with salt and enough ice water to cover all. Let stand for one hour and drain. Combine remaining ingredients and bring to a boil. Add drained vegetable mixture and return to a rapid boil. Pack in sterile jars, cover with juice and seal.

TOMATOES AND GREEN CHILIES

1 gallon tomatoes, peeled and quartered
5 large onions, chopped
1½ cups jalapeno peppers, chopped
1 cup vinegar
1/4 cup canning salt

Bring all to a boil and cook for 30 minutes, or until onions are tender. Put in hot, sterile pint jars. Seal and process in hot water bath for 15 minutes. Makes 10 pints. For cheese dip, use 1 pound processed cheese to 1 pint tomatoes and green chilies. THIS IS VERY HOT. For milder sauce, use only 3/4 cup peppers.

CHILI SAUCE

4 large green bell peppers, chopped
2 large red bell peppers, chopped
3 medium onions, chopped
2 Tablespoons chili powder
1/2 cup oil
3 cups tomato puree
3/4 cup chicken broth
3 canned jalapeno peppers, finely chopped
1 Tablespoon jalapeno juice from can

Saute onion and peppers in oil until tender and clear. Add chili powder and cook slowly for 5 minutes. Add puree and broth and simmer for 10 minutes. Add jalapeno juice and simmer another 5 minutes. Let cool completely and freeze in desired size containers.

QUICK HOT DOG RELISH

1/2 cup pickle relish
1/2 cup prepared mustard

Mix together, place in jar and keep refrigerated.

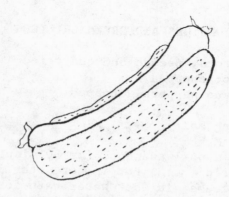

OTHER DESIRABLES

OTHER DESIRABLES

Miscellaneous

ERMANENT

BEEF OR VENISON JERKY

MISCELLANEOUS

3 pounds round steak or venison steak
1½ Tablespoons salt
1/2 cup warm water
1/2 cup soy sauce
1/2 cup Worcestershire sauce
1/2 cup prepared barbeque sauce

Cut meat a scant 1/2-inch thick and with grain in 3/4-inch strips. Mix remaining ingredients in order, making sure to dissolve salt in water. Soak meat for 4 hours stirring strips in sauce to turn over. Place strips of meat on paper towels for 5 minutes, then put on rack in oven. Turn heat on at this time to 130° and cook for 8½ hours, leaving door slightly ajar. Open oven door, turn off heat and let dry in oven for 8 more hours. Store in bags.

GRANOLA

6 cups old fashioned oats
1 cup wheat germ
1 cup dry powdered milk
1 cup raw sunflower seeds
1 cup sesame seeds
1 cup coconut
1/2 cup slivered almonds
1/2 cup shelled pumpkin seeds
1/3 cup oil
1/3 cup honey
1 cup water or apple juice

Heat oil, honey and water and mix with other ingredients until moistened. Spread in two 9X13 cake pans and bake in 325° oven for approximately 30 minutes or until light brown and crisp. Stir often. After mixture is cooled, any or all of the following may be added: raisins, peanuts, dried fruits, or chocolate chips.

236

MAYONNAISE

2 egg yolks
1 teaspoon salt
1 teaspoon dry mustard
2 cups oil
3 Tablespoons lemon juice
1 teaspoon sugar
1/2 teaspoon paprika

Beat eggs with 1 Tablespoon lemon juice with electric mixer. Add salt, sugar, mustard and paprika beating until well blended. Add oil, just a little at a time, beating constantly until very thick. Oil can be added faster as mayonnaise thickens. When very thick, add remaining lemon juice, then add remaining oil slowly still beating constantly until well mixed. Be sure you are beating this mixture constantly with your electric mixer once you start.

SWEETENED CONDENSED MILK

1 cup dry milk
2/3 cup granulated sugar
1/3 cup boiling water
3 Tablespoons softened butter

Mix all ingredients together in blender and blend until smooth. Must be kept refrigerated.

BANANA ICE CREAM

3 eggs, lightly beaten
2 cups sugar
1 Tablespoon vanilla
3 medium bananas, ripe and mashed
1 quart milk
1 pint half and half
1 pint whipping cream

Mix eggs, sugar and bananas well and set aside. Combine milk and cream, stir in banana mixture and mix well. Add vanilla last along with enough whole milk to make a gallon. Freeze.

COUNTRY STYLE VANILLA ICE CREAM

4 eggs
3 cups sugar
1/4 teapoon salt
5 cups milk
1 Tablespoon vanilla
4 cartons whipping cream

Beat eggs until frothy. Slowly add sugar and beat until thickened. Add cream, vanilla, milk and salt, and beat well. Pour into freezer can and add enough whole milk to fill freezer can. Stir well and freeze.

TUTTI FRUTTI ICE CREAM

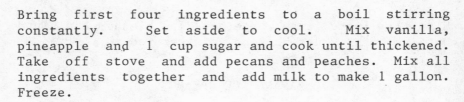

2½ cups sugar
1 Tablespoon flour
1 pint milk
4 eggs, beaten
1 teaspoon vanilla
1 small can crushed pineapple
1 cup sugar
1 cup pecans, chopped
1 large can peaches, drained and mashed

Bring first four ingredients to a boil stirring constantly. Set aside to cool. Mix vanilla, pineapple and 1 cup sugar and cook until thickened. Take off stove and add pecans and peaches. Mix all ingredients together and add milk to make 1 gallon. Freeze.

FROSTED GRAPES

fresh bunches of grapes
1 egg white
granulated sugar

Sift sugar several times until very fine. Brush grapes with egg whites then lightly sift sugar over grapes to coat. Refrigerate. These are very pretty and great for garnishing.

238

MUSHROOM TOAST

1 pound mushrooms
1/4 cup butter
3 Tablespoons flour
2 cups milk
salt and pepper

Wash and slice mushrooms. Cook in butter until done.
Dissolve flour in 1/2 cup milk and pour into skillet
with mushrooms.   Add rest of milk, stir and cook
about 5 to 10 minutes. Serve over toasted bread.

FROZEN STRAWBERRY PRESERVES

2 cups crushed strawberries
4 cups sugar
1 box fruit pectin
3/4 cup water

Mix strawberries and sugar and let set 1 hour,
stirring several times to dissolve sugar. Dissolve
fruit pectin in water and boil for 1 minute. Add this
to strawberries and stir for 3 minutes. Put in
sterile jars and cover with cloth until jelled. Seal
and refrigerate or freeze.

PEPPER JELLY

1 cup ground bell pepper
2 Tablespoons ground hot peppers
1½ cups cider vinegar
6½ cups sugar
1 6-oz. bottle liquid fruit pectin
green food coloring

Mix everything except fruit pectin in saucepan and
bring to a boil. Let boil for 5 minutes, remove from
heat and add fruit pectin stirring until mixture
starts to jell. Pour into sterile jelly jars and
seal. (This is good spooned over a brick of cream
cheese and served with ginger snaps).

239

CHRISTMAS FRAGRANCE

1 can apple juice
1 can pickling spices
1 can whole cloves
1 box cinnamon sticks

Mix together in crock pot. Add water to fill container, bring to a boil and turn to simmer. Lasts about 1 week. Strain out spices and reuse adding fresh water and juices. **NON-EDIBLE**

DOUGH ORNAMENTS

4 cups flour
1 cup salt
1½ cups water

Mix together and turn out on foil covered cookie sheet. Knead about 10 minutes. Dough will dry quickly so it must be kept wrapped in plastic wrap. Roll out dough and cut ornaments. Make hole for hanging or place hanger in dough before baking. Bake at 350° for 45 minutes or until light brown. Cool and paint. For high gloss, a clear varnish can be used over paint. **NON-EDIBLE**

KID'S PLAY DOUGH

2 cups flour
1/2 cup salt
1 Tablespoon oil
water

Mix first three ingredients together. Add water a little at a time until you have a good dough consistency. Add food coloring and work until smooth. **NON-EDIBLE.**

SOAK FOR WHITE CLOTHING

1 gallon hot water
1 cup automatic dishwashing powder
1/4 cup liquid chlorine bleach

Mix well in large plastic or stainless pan. (Do not use aluminum). Soak whites for 30 minutes and wash as usual. For cottons use hot water, for synthetics use warm water. **NON-EDIBLE**

OTHER DESIRABLES

A

245

Make Checks Payable and Mail to: **S-M-L, Inc.**
P.O. Box 243
DeWitt, AR 72042

Please send me _____ copies of **THE FARMER'S DAUGHTERS**
@ $17.50 each plus $3.00 postage and handling per book. All Arkansas
residents add 8.125% ($1.42) sales tax.
Enclosed is my check for $_____.

NAME _____
ADDRESS _____
CITY _____STATE _____ZIP_____

Make Checks Payable and Mail to: **S-M-L, Inc.**
P.O. Box 243
DeWitt, AR 72042

Please send me _____ copies of **THE FARMER'S DAUGHTERS**
@ $17.50 each plus $3.00 postage and handling per book. All Arkansas
residents add 8.125% ($1.42) sales tax.
Enclosed is my check for $_____.

NAME _____
ADDRESS_____
CITY _____STATE _____ZIP_____

Make Checks Payable and Mail to: **S-M-L, Inc.**
P.O. Box 243
DeWitt, AR 72042

Please send me _____ copies of **THE FARMER'S DAUGHTERS**
@ $17.50 each plus $3.00 postage and handling per book. All Arkansas
residents add 8.125% ($1.42) sales tax.
Enclosed is my check for $_____.

NAME _____
ADDRESS _____
CITY _____STATE _____ZIP_____

Reorder Additional Copies